TWENTIETH CENTURY
INTERPRETATIONS

MAYNARD MACK, *Series Editor*
Yale University

NOW AVAILABLE
Collections of Critical Essays
ON

TWENTIETH CENTURY
INTERPRETATIONS
OF
THE GREAT GATSBY

TWENTIETH CENTURY INTERPRETATIONS
OF
THE
GREAT GATSBY

A Collection of Critical Essays

Edited by
ERNEST LOCKRIDGE

Prentice-Hall, Inc. *Englewood Cliffs, N. J.*

A SPECTRUM BOOK

Copyright © 1968 by Prentice-Hall, Inc., Englewood Cliffs, New Jersey. A
SPECTRUM BOOK. All rights reserved. No part of this book may be reproduced
in any form or by any means without permission in writing from the publisher.
Library of Congress Catalog Card Number 68-15490. Printed in the United States
of America.

Current printing (last number):
11

Contents

Part Two—*View Points*

Introduction

by Ernest Lockridge

F. Scott Fitzgerald was born September 24, 1896, in St. Paul, Minnesota, a "Westerner" like the major characters in *The Great Gatsby,* considered by most critics his finest novel. He attended Princeton University, where he formed friendships with Edmund Wilson and John Peale Bishop. Leaving Princeton in 1917, part-way through his senior year, he served two years in the stateside army as a second lieutenant. In September, 1919, Maxwell Perkins, the famous editor who later worked with Ernest Hemingway and Thomas Wolfe, accepted *This Side of Paradise* for Scribner's. The novel was published March 26, 1920. "In a daze I told the Scribner Company that I didn't expect my novel to sell more than twenty thousand copies," Fitzgerald wrote, "and when the laughter died away I was told that a sale of five thousand was excellent for a first novel. I think it was a week after publication that it passed the twenty thousand mark, but I took myself so seriously that I didn't even think it was funny." [1] One week after publication, Fitzgerald married a lovely, brilliant girl named Zelda Sayre.

Like Byron, Fitzgerald became overnight a famous writer, and the Fitzgeralds became one of the Twenties' most notorious couples. "The offices of editors and publishers were open to me," Fitzgerald wrote of this period, "impresarios begged plays, the movies panted for screen material. . . . I, who knew less of New York than any reporter of six months standing and less of its society than any hall-room boy in a Ritz stag line, was pushed into the position not only of spokesman for the time but of the typical product of that same moment." He and Zelda were "news": "a dive into a civic fountain, a casual brush with the law, was enough to get us into the gossip columns, and we were quoted on a variety of subjects we knew nothing about." [2] Their only child, a daughter, was born in 1921. But the marriage grew chaotic. Beginning in 1928, Zelda tried desperately and unsuccessfully to become a dancer. Her first major breakdown occurred in 1930, and by 1934 she had become insane. She died in March, 1947, in a sanitarium

[1] F. Scott Fitzgerald, *The Crack-Up,* ed. Edmund Wilson (New York, 1945), p. 88.
[2] *Crack-Up,* pp. 26-7.

1

fire, seven years after Fitzgerald's own death. In a 1938 letter to his
daughter, Fitzgerald judged his early life and marriage:

> When I was your age I lived with a great dream. The dream grew and
> I learned how to speak of it and make people listen. Then the dream
> divided one day when I decided to marry your mother after all, even
> though I knew she was spoiled and meant no good to me. I was sorry
> immediately I had married her but, being patient in those days, made
> the best of it and got to love her in another way. You came along and
> for a long time we made quite a lot of happiness out of our lives. But I
> was a man divided—she wanted me to work too much for *her* and not
> enough for my dream. She realized too late that work was dignity, and the
> only dignity, and tried to atone for it by working herself, but it was too
> late and she broke and is broken forever.[3]

With *This Side of Paradise* a bestseller, Fitzgerald achieved financial success as a novelist and writer of short stories, though his
earnings barely kept pace with his extravagance. In March, 1922, Scribner's published his second novel, *The Beautiful and Damned,* which
also sold well. But in November, 1923, Fitzgerald's play, *The Vegeta-
ble,* opened in Atlantic City, and most of the first night audience
walked out. "It was a colossal frost," Fitzgerald wrote. "I wanted to
stop the show and say it was all a mistake but the actors struggled he-
roically on." [4] The play failed.

Fitzgerald did not achieve critical success until April, 1925, when
The Great Gatsby was published. Though brilliant in individual passages, his first two novels were unselective and uncontrolled; a friend
of Fitzgerald's facetiously labeled *This Side of Paradise*—into which
Fitzgerald dumped undergraduate essays, sketches, short stories, and
poems—the collected works of F. Scott Fitzgerald. The novels lack
overall patterning and structure. Writing *Gatsby,* however, Fitzgerald
followed the advice he later gave his long-winded contemporary,
Thomas Wolfe: "I think I could make out a good case for your neces-
sity to cultivate an alter ego, a more conscious artist in you. . . . The
novel of selected incidents has this to be said: that the great writer like
Flaubert has consciously left out the stuff that Bill or Joe (in his case,
Zola) will come along and say presently. He will say only the things
that he alone sees. So *Madame Bovary* becomes eternal while Zola already rocks with age. . . ." [5] *Gatsby* fulfilled the promise which Edmund Wilson and Paul Rosenfeld, among others, had clearly sensed

[3] F. Scott Fitzgerald, *Letters to his Daughter,* ed. Andrew Turnbull (New York,
1965), p. 51.
  [4] Andrew Turnbull, *Scott Fitzgerald* (New York, 1962), p. 140.
  [5] F. Scott Fitzgerald, *The Letters of F. Scott Fitzgerald,* ed. Andrew Turnbull
(New York, 1963), p. 552.

in Fitzgerald, though the novel did not sell nearly so well as his first two.

Fitzgerald did not publish his fourth novel, *Tender is the Night,* until April, 1934. He expected critics to hail it as his best novel, and a few did; but by 1934 the depression was five years old, and literary fashion had shifted to the proletarian novel, which dealt with the hardship of farmers, migrant laborers, factory workers, and their like. Critics largely denounced *Tender is the Night,* an excellent novel, as "a rather irritating type of *chic*"[6]; it did not sell. Meanwhile, Fitzgerald supported himself by writing short stories and working sporadically for Hollywood.

In 1935, "ten years this side of forty-nine," Fitzgerald "suddenly realized that [he] had prematurely cracked." [7] Alcoholism, a problem for him since the early 1920's, along with his wife's insanity and the failure of *Tender is the Night,* contributed to his crack-up. Fitzgerald has written brilliantly and movingly about this two-year period when his dream failed utterly and he was no longer able to assert his identity upon the world, to achieve that moment "when the fulfilled future and the wistful past were mingled in a single gorgeous moment—when life was literally a dream." [8] He said that prior to his crack-up "life was something you dominated if you were any good. Life yielded easily to intelligence and effort, or to what proportion could be mustered of both"—there were no gods, and life had meaning in proportion only to one's vitality for asserting meaning upon it.[9] When Fitzgerald's vitality failed, meaning failed—the meaning of all human effort, even writing[10]—and he fell victim to acedia:

> a feeling that I was standing at twilight on a deserted range, with an empty rifle in my hands and the targets down. No problem set—simply a silence with only the sound of my own breathing.
>
> In this silence there was a vast irresponsibility toward every obligation, a deflation of all my values. A passionate belief in order, a disregard of motives or consequences in favor of guess work and prophecy, a feeling that craft and industry would have a place in any world—one by one, these and other convictions were swept away.[11]

In 1937, while Fitzgerald was writing for motion pictures, he met Sheilah Graham, whose influence revitalized his last years. But physical and mental exhaustion proved overwhelming. During his final year

[6] Arthur Mizener, *The Far Side of Paradise* (Boston, 1951), p. 238.
[7] *Crack-Up,* p. 70.
[8] *Crack-Up,* p. 90.
[9] *Crack-Up,* pp. 69, 74-5.
[10] *Crack-Up,* p. 78.
[11] *Crack-Up,* p. 78.

of life, he consciously raced death to complete his fifth novel, *The Last Tycoon*. "Look!" he wrote his daughter on October 31, 1939, "I have begun to write something that is maybe great, and I'm going to be absorbed in it four or six months." [12] He wrote Maxwell Perkins, December 13, 1940, "The novel progresses—in fact progresses fast. I'm not going to stop now till I finish a first draft which will be sometime after the 15th of January." [13] But eight days later, December 21, he died following two heart attacks, the novel still uncompleted.

Part of *The Great Gatsby*'s lasting significance derives from the extent to which Fitzgerald recognizes and grapples with some basic problems of the twentieth century. In 1936, during his crack-up, Fitzgerald wrote, "let me make a general observation—the test of a first-rate intelligence is the ability to hold two opposed ideas in the mind at the same time and still retain the ability to function. One should, for example, be able to see that things are hopeless and yet be determined to make them otherwise." [14] This "test" would be unnecessary—would, in fact, be perversely wrongheaded—if man could regard his universe as a genuine unity. If there existed some static ultimate principle, metaphysical or theological—Platonic forms, say, or a Christian God —which unified seemingly "opposed ideas," then opposed ideas would be revealed as figments of an intelligence which was merely second-rate. But like so many other first-rate intelligences of the twentieth century—philosophers, scientists, and artists acutely sensitive to the problems of the age—Fitzgerald found it necessary to cope with a universe placed well "this side of paradise," where the "ultimate" principles of the wise appear to be nonexistent and therefore give no comfort. "Do not let me hear," T. S. Eliot insists, "Of the wisdom of old men." [15] In James Joyce's *Ulysses* (1922), when the officious Mr. Deasey advises Stephen Dedalus, "Put money in thy purse," Stephen destroys the advice by murmuring, "Iago," the maxim's real perpetrator.[16] "What makes the old such an Arab tea party is their ideas," says a character in Aldous Huxley's *Point Counter Point* (1928), that scrapbook of the modern mind. "I simply cannot believe that thick arteries will ever make me believe in God and Morals and all the rest of it. I came out of the chrysalis during the war, when the bottom had been knocked out of everything. I don't see how our grandchildren could possibly knock it out any more thoroughly than it was knocked out

[12] *The Letters of F. Scott Fitzgerald*, p. 61.
[13] *The Letters*, p. 270.
[14] *Crack-Up*, p. 69.
[15] T. S. Eliot, "East Coker," *The Complete Poems and Plays 1909-1950* (New York, 1962), p. 125.
[16] James Joyce, *Ulysses* (New York: Modern Library, 1961), p. 30.

then." [17] To Stephen Dedalus, God is "a shout in the street," simply the manifestation of blind process without progress; "God becomes man becomes fish becomes barnacle goose becomes featherbed mountain," in a "world without end," without order, purpose, or meaning.[18] Eliot's *Waste Land* (1922), which Fitzgerald knew thoroughly, describes a multiverse of "fragments" and "ruins":

> What is that sound high in the air
> Murmur of maternal lamentation
> Who are those hooded hordes swarming
> Over endless plains, stumbling in cracked earth
> Ringed by the flat horizon only
> What is the city over the mountains
> Cracks and reforms and bursts in the violet air
> Falling towers
> Jerusalem Athens Alexandria
> Vienna London
> Unreal [19]

Man's universe itself has cracked up.

Intelligent man in the twentieth century may no longer have great confidence that the structure of human thinking and the structure of reality coincide. "Strangeness creeps in," writes Albert Camus in *The Myth of Sisyphus* (1942), when we perceive

> to what a degree a stone is foreign and irreducible to us, with what intensity nature or a landscape can negate us. At the heart of all beauty lies something inhuman, and these hills, the softness of the sky, the outline of these trees at this very minute lose the illusory meaning with which we had clothed them, henceforth more remote than a lost paradise. The primitive hostility of the world rises up to face us across millennia. For a second we cease to understand it because for centuries we have understood in it solely the images and designs that we had attributed to it beforehand, because henceforth we lack the power to make use of that artifice. The world evades us because it becomes itself again.[20]

Contemporary physics indicates that even the laws of classical physics, so lucid and "permanent," by which it seemed man could reduce nature to himself, are merely convenient fictions invented by the human mind and imposed upon a nature which refuses to conform. In *Science and the Modern World* (1925), Alfred North Whitehead writes:

[17] Aldous Huxley, *Point Counter Point* (New York: Avon, n.d.), pp. 142-3.
[18] Joyce, pp. 34, 50, 37.
[19] Eliot, p. 48.
[20] Albert Camus, *The Myth of Sisyphus*, tr. Justin O'Brien (New York, 1955), p. 11.

The note of the present epoch is that so many complexities have developed regarding material space, time, and energy, that the simple security of the old orthodox assumptions has vanished. It is obvious that they will not do as Newton left them, or even as Clerk Maxwell left them.[21]

A "Platonic" world-view of fixed values and laws—a world-view where "the One remains, the many change and pass," where the past repeats itself in cycles and the future is logically and predictably determined by the past—gives way, now, to a "Heraclitean" world-view, a dynamic, unpredictable multiverse of process and flux where you "cannot step twice into the same stream." In *The Philosophical Impact of Contemporary Physics*, Mileč Čapek states:

Contemporary physics in its implications returns by devious and complicated ways to the evidence of our immediate experience . . . to . . . *a really growing world with genuine novelties.* . . .

In such a growing world every present event is undoubtedly caused, though not necessitated by its own past. For as long as it is not yet present, its specific character remains uncertain. . . . [Only] its presentness . . . creates its specificity, i.e., brings an end to its uncertainty, by eliminating all other possible features incompatible with it. Thus every present event is by its own nature an *act of selection* ending the hesitation of reality between various possibilities.[22]

This "affirmation of *real novelties* in the physical world" means that just as it is impossible to project the future, so it is impossible to repeat the past. "Each moment in virtue of its own authentic freshness is unique and unrepeatable. Thus novelty implies irreversibility." [23] Or as a great artist puts it:

> There is, it seems to us,
> At best, only a limited value
> In the knowledge derived from experience.
> The knowledge imposes a pattern, and falsifies.
> For the pattern is new in every moment
> And every moment is a new and shocking
> Valuation of all we have been.[24]

[21] Alfred North Whitehead, *Science and the Modern World* (New York, 1948), p. 106.

[22] Mileč Čapek, *The Philosophical Impact of Contemporary Physics* (Princeton, N.J., 1961), p. 340.

[23] Čapek, p. 344.

[24] Eliot, p. 125.

"Can't repeat the past?" cries Gatsby "incredulously" to Nick Carraway, narrator of *The Great Gatsby.* "Why of course you can!" (111) [25] Gatsby has bootlegged a fortune in order to buy back the past, to recover the time five years before when "he kissed [Daisy Fay] and forever wed his unutterable visions to her perishable breath," when "at his lips' touch she blossomed for him like a flower and the incarnation was complete." (112) In that past moment, Gatsby seems to have achieved no mere holding of "two opposed ideas in the mind at the same time," but a triumph over chaos: the total unity of "forever" with perishing, vision with breath, spirit with matter—a momentary incarnation which halts and transcends the process of time. Even if the moment is lost, Gatsby believes he can recover it and "blot out . . . five years of [his own] unwavering devotion" as if they had never existed." (110) But at the very moment of "incarnation" "one autumn night" in Louisville "when the leaves [are] falling," a loss occurs: "[Gatsby's] mind," Nick says, will "never romp again like the mind of God." Shortly after Daisy has married Tom Buchanan, Gatsby revisits Louisville, attempts to recover the moment, and fails: "He stretched out his hand desperately as if to snatch only a wisp of air, to save a fragment of the spot that she had made lovely for him. But it was all going by too fast now for his blurred eyes and he knew that he had lost that part of it, the freshest and the best, forever." (153) Of Gatsby's first meeting with Daisy after five years, Nick Carraway writes:

> I saw that the expression of bewilderment had come back into Gatsby's face, as though a faint doubt had occurred to him as to the quality of his present happiness. Almost five years! There must have been moments even that afternoon when Daisy tumbled short of his dreams—not through her own fault, but because of the colossal vitality of his illusion. It had gone beyond her, beyond everything. He had thrown himself into it with a creative passion, adding to it all the time, decking it out with every bright feather that drifted his way. (97)

In the end, a victim of time and its own fictionality, the dream dies. Almost anticlimactically, Gatsby's death follows.

Yet with this knowledge of failure before him, Nick Carraway affirms the value of Gatsby, who represents everything for which Nick has "an unaffected scorn"; and he affirms the value of Gatsby's failed, unreal dream. "Gatsby turned out all right at the end; it is what preyed on Gatsby, what foul dust floated in the wake of his dreams that temporarily closed out my interest in the abortive sorrows and short-

[25] All references are to F. Scott Fitzgerald, *The Great Gatsby* (New York: Scribner's paperback, 1953).

winded elations of men." (2) It is the purpose of this essay to discover
the meaning of Nick's, and by implication Fitzgerald's, affirmation.

During the chaotic and violent party in Myrtle Wilson's New York
apartment, Nick thinks: "high over the city our line of yellow windows
must have contributed their share of human secrecy to the casual
watcher in the darkening streets, and I was him too, looking up and
wondering. I was within and without, *simultaneously enchanted and
repelled by the inexhaustible variety of life.*" (36, italics added) It is
the enchantment of life's "inexhaustible variety" which makes Nick
"inclined to reserve all judgments." "Reserving judgments," he says,
"is a matter of infinite hope." (1) To some extent, he possesses, like
Gatsby, a "heightened sensitivity to the promises of life, as if he were
related to one of those intricate machines that register earthquakes ten
thousand miles away." (2) It is, however, the repellent nature of life's
variety which makes Nick assert that his tolerance "has a limit."
"When I came back from the East last autumn I felt that I wanted
the world to be in uniform at a sort of moral attention forever." (2)
"Life," he says elsewhere, "is much more successfully looked at from
a single window, after all" (4)—as if "the inexhaustible variety of life,"
by itself, were chaos which man must somehow limit in order to survive. In this context, Gatsby's smile becomes significant: it "[faces]—
or [seems] to face—the whole external world for an instant, and then
[concentrates] on *you. . . .*" (48) From its opening pages, *The Great
Gatsby* embodies "two opposed ideas," a polarity which can be vari-
ously labeled: "the inexhaustible variety of life" versus "life . . .
much more successfully looked at from a single window," "earthquakes
ten thousand miles away" versus "one of those intricate machines"
which man constructs to register them, "foul dust" versus "dreams";
and, more generally, plenitude versus limitation, matter versus spirit,
body versus mind, process versus stasis, nonhuman chaos versus human
order.

Like Proteus, chaos in *The Great Gatsby* assumes many forms. "Foul
dust" finds its greatest extension, of course, in the "valley of ashes,"
that deliberate reflection of Eliot's waste land. (cf. 24) Here "spiritless"
men (25) become indistinguishable from the spiritless landscape; the
nonhuman defeats and absorbs the human. "This is a valley of ashes—
a fantastic farm where ashes grow like wheat into ridges and hills and
grotesque gardens; where ashes take the forms of houses and chimneys
and rising smoke and, finally, with a transcendent effort, of men who
move dimly and already crumbling through the powdery air." (23) It
is from this landscape that Myrtle Wilson, Tom Buchanan's mistress,
symbolically appears, for she is body without spirit: "Her face, above
a spotted dress of dark blue crêpe-de-chine, contained no facet or gleam

of beauty, but there was an immediately perceptible vitality about her as if the nerves of her body were continually smouldering." (25) Like the dog Tom buys for her, she is a bitch; Tom, who keeps a string of ponies, is a stud: in the world of *Gatsby,* man who resigns himself to his nonhuman environment becomes like the beast. Or like inanimate objects: "When I was here last," says a woman at Gatsby's party, "I tore my gown on a chair, and he asked me my name and address. . . ." (43) Or fragmented body-parts: the butler, say, reduced to his nose, (14) or Wolfsheim to his own "expressive nose" (70) and his cufflinks made from "finest specimens of human molars." (73) Like Eliot's *Prufrock,* with its detached claws, arms, and heads, like *The Waste Land,* where all connections have broken down ("I can connect nothing with nothing," laments a Thames maiden[26]), Fitzgerald's world here seems to lie in fragments. In one scene, "the gardens of Versailles," "several old copies of *Town Tattler . . .* together with a copy of *Simon Called Peter,* and some of the small scandal magazines of Broadway," a dog and a tin of dogbiscuits decomposing in milk, "a sticky bob of red hair," and "feet"—all lie strewn disconnectedly about. (29-31) "Truth" is what one hears from three people. (20) Images of blindness predominate: "The little dog was sitting on the table looking with blind eyes through the smoke" (37); "Blinded by the glare of the headlights. . . ." (55) "After Gatsby's death," Nick says, "the East was haunted for me . . . , distorted beyond my eyes' power of correction." (178) "God sees everything," says the demented Wilson. (160) But the "God" to which Wilson refers, the God of this world, is "an advertisement," the disembodied, blind eyes of Doctor T. J. Eckleburg:

> above the gray land and the spasms of bleak dust which drift endlessly over it, you perceive, after a moment, the eyes of Doctor T. J. Eckleburg. The eyes of Doctor T. J. Eckleburg are blue and gigantic—their retinas are one yard high. They look out of no face, but, instead, from a pair of enormous yellow spectacles which pass over a non-existent nose. Evidently some wild wag of an oculist set them there to fatten his practice in the borough of Queens, and then sank down himself into eternal blindness, or forgot them and moved away. But his eyes, dimmed a little by many paintless days under sun and rain, brood over the solemn dumping ground. (23)

" 'Civilization's going to pieces,' [breaks] out Tom violently. 'I've gotten to be a terrible pessimist about things.' " (13) And later: "I read somewhere that the sun's getting hotter every year. . . . It seems that pretty soon the earth's going to fall into the sun—or wait a minute —it's just the opposite—the sun's getting colder every year." (118)

---

[26] Eliot, p. 46.

"Stale ideas" perhaps (21)—but the world of the novel does appear to teeter at the edge of apocalypse, a total annihilation in which much of mankind willingly participates.

Perhaps because it seems so intensely real where almost everything else seems unclear and unreal, or because it contrasts so cleanly with the restless, drifting lives of people in the waste land, violence possesses a fatal attraction for man in the novel. Tom Buchanan, arrogant and cruel, seeks "the dramatic turbulence of some irrecoverable football game" (6) and finds its surrogate in his violent affair with Myrtle Wilson ("Making a short deft movement, Tom Buchanan broke her nose with his open hand." 37). Even Nick Carraway, the gentle narrator, finds war so exciting that he "[comes] back restless. Instead of being the warm center of the world, the Middle West now [seems] like the ragged edge of the universe. . . ."(3) Violence dogs the novel in fights, murders, and accidents. "I can't forget so long as I live the night they shot Rosy Rosenthal there," Wolfsheim says. "They shot him three times in his full belly and drove away." Nick thinks only four of the murderers were electrocuted, but Wolfsheim casually corrects him: "Five, with Becker." (70-1) "A week after I left Santa Barbara Tom ran into a wagon on the Ventura road one night and ripped a front wheel off his car," Nick recounts. "The girl who was with him got into the papers, too, because her arm was broken. . . ." (78) Dan Cody, Gatsby's early mentor, brings "back to the Eastern seaboard the savage violence of the frontier brothel and saloon." (101) ". . . Myrtle Wilson, her life violently extinguished, [kneels] in the road and [mingles] her thick dark blood with the dust . . . her left breast . . . swinging loose like a flap. . . . The mouth [is] wide open and ripped at the corners, as though she had choked a little in giving up the tremendous vitality she had stored so long." (136) Wilson murders Gatsby, then commits suicide, in what Nick describes as a "holocaust." (163) Daisy speaks of fire and flood as acts "of God" (107); and it seems in the novel as if the meaningless, nonhuman process of destruction and change were indeed the very nature of things.

Either man willingly delivers himself up to destruction, the novel implies, or he attempts, if only in vain, to preserve himself. Gatsby's relationship to his parties appears iconic of this attempt at self-preservation. The party which Nick describes in Chapter III rapidly disintegrates into violence and disorder. Knowledge becomes imprecise, relationships ambiguous: " 'She had a fight with a man who says he's her husband,' explained a girl at my elbow. . . . Most of the remaining women were now having fights with men said to be their husbands." (52)

Fifty feet from the door a dozen headlights illuminated a bizarre and tumultuous scene. In the ditch beside the road, right side up, but violently shorn of one wheel, rested a new coupé which had left Gatsby's drive not two minutes before. The sharp jut of a wall accounted for the detachment of the wheel, which was now getting considerable attention from half a dozen curious chauffeurs. However, as they had left their cars blocking the road, a harsh, discordant din from those in the rear had been audible for some time, and added to the already violent confusion of the scene. (54)

Isolated from this confusion, Gatsby preserves inviolate a small island of order. Nick remarks, "I wondered if the fact that he was not drinking helped to set him off from his guests, for it seemed to me that he grew more correct as the fraternal hilarity increased." (50) As the "caterwauling horns" reach a crescendo, Gatsby stands "on the porch, his hand up in a formal gesture of farewell," (56) "concealing his incorruptible dream, as he [waves] them goodbye" (155)—a dream of human order amid chaos.

Gatsby's dream divides into three basic and related parts: the desire to repeat the past, the desire for money, and the desire for incarnation of "unutterable visions" in the material earth.

If the nature of things is irreversible change, if "each moment in virtue of its own authentic freshness is unique and unrepeatable," if "there is . . . at best, only a limited value in the knowledge derived from experience," the remembered past nonetheless gives man a satisfying and necessary illusion of process forever stopped. Thinking back upon a past event, man can say: "It *was* thus-and-so; it will always have been thus-and-so." Memory by itself gives man a handhold upon reality, a node of order and stability within flux, like one of McKee's photographic stills. If man could somehow go further and repeat the past, he would control concrete reality, because he would unify it with the abstraction in his mind. The meaning of the past would *be* the meaning of the present, and nonhuman, meaningless chaos would cease.

Several characters in the novel desire to repeat a significant past preserved in memory. As a football end for Yale, Tom Buchanan reached "such an acute limited excellence at twenty-one that everything afterward savors of anticlimax"; Nick feels, as mentioned earlier, "that Tom would drift on forever seeking, a little wistfully, for the dramatic turbulence of some irrecoverable football game." (6) Nick himself, at novel's end, returns west in hope, it seems, of repeating his "vivid" memory "of coming back West from prep school and later from college at Christmas time":

When we pulled out into the winter night and the real snow, our snow, began to stretch out beside us and twinkle against the windows, and the dim lights of small Wisconsin stations moved by, a sharp wild brace came suddenly into the air. We drew in deep breaths of it as we walked back from dinner through the cold vestibules, unutterably aware of our identity with this country for one strange hour, before we melted indistinguishably into it again. (176-7).

It is significant that Nick's memory is of "one strange hour" when man and nature seem to unite with conscious human meaning, before nature reabsorbs man. Gatsby, of course, wishes to recover intact his first, fresh love for Daisy, and this too is impossible. Process triumphs; the repeatable past proves a fiction. There is, for example, the undeniable fact of Daisy's child by Tom: "Gatsby . . . kept looking at the child with surprise. I don't think he had ever really believed in its existence before." (117) Daisy herself cannot admit that she never loved Tom and therefore cannot wipe out "forever" everything which has happened during five years: " 'Oh, you want too much!' she cried to Gatsby. 'I love you now—isn't that enough? I can't help what's past.' She began to sob helplessly. 'I did love him once—but I loved you too.' " (133) The past, forever left behind, is represented by the outdated timetable for July 5, 1922, "old . . . now, disintegrating at its folds," on which Nick wrote down the names of those who attended Gatsby's parties; it should be noticed that many of these partygoers are later killed or maimed.

Writing his ambitious poem *The Bridge* during the same decade that Fitzgerald wrote *The Great Gatsby,* Hart Crane portrayed the search for America's present and future meaning as a search for the meaning of America's past; the poem attempts to plunge back into America's "tribal morn" and achieve union with the American earth, personified by the historical Pocahontas. The search fails. Like Crane, Fitzgerald expands this failed search beyond individual characters, expands it to include America and, by implication, all mankind. If, for "a transitory enchanted moment" when Dutch sailors first beheld the new world, man's mind and the world united, it was "for the last time in history." (182)

Money represents another attempt—more debased, perhaps—to order concrete reality by abstract idea. Contrary to common misconception, money is a purely human abstraction, a value and a power arbitrarily conferred by the human mind upon the world. In *Gatsby,* money gives man great, if temporary, control. Much of Tom's power derives from his immense wealth: "He'd brought down a string of polo ponies from Lake Forest," Nick remarks. "It was hard to realize that a man in my own generation was wealthy enough to do that." (6) More profoundly, money appears strong enough to freeze the past, to halt process: "Gatsby was overwhelmingly aware of the youth and mystery that wealth imprisons and preserves, of the freshness of many clothes, and of Daisy, gleaming like silver, safe and proud above the hot struggles of the poor." (150) But this strength buckles. Whether Fitzgerald consciously designed it thus or not, money gives Gatsby control over three of the four medieval "elements": his "gorgeous car" masters earth and, symbolically, air ("with fenders spread like wings we scattered light through half Astoria." [68]), his "hydroplane" masters air and water. What he finally cannot master is the fourth element, fire, Heraclitean symbol of change, which metaphorically destroys him. It is after "almost the last, certainly the warmest" day of the summer, in an atmosphere of "broiling" heat (114), that Gatsby dies. Summer moves brutally into fall, life into death. "Our eyes lifted over the rose-beds and the hot lawn and the weedy refuse of the dog-days alongshore." Heat creates disorder, and the human voice vainly attempts to "[mould] its senselessness into forms." (118-19) The failure of money, a mere concept, to halt process is prefigured when Nick first enters New York City in Gatsby's car:

> Over the great bridge, with the sunlight through the girders making a constant flicker upon the moving cars, with the city rising up across the river in white heaps and sugar lumps *all built with a wish out of non-olfactory money.* The city seen from the Queensboro Bridge is always the city seen for the first time, in its first wild promise of all the mystery and the beauty in the world.
>
> *A dead man passed us in a hearse heaped with blooms.* . . . (69, italics added)

It is on the day of incredible heat that the world races forever past Gatsby's dream:

> he began to talk excitedly to Daisy, denying everything, defending his name against accusations that had not been made. But with every word she was drawing further and further into herself, so he gave that up, and only the dead dream fought on as the afternoon slipped away, trying to touch what was no longer tangible, struggling unhappily, undespairingly, toward that lost voice across the room. (135)

In the evening, Daisy, driving Gatsby's car, kills Myrtle Wilson. The next day in what, as mentioned above, Nick terms a "holocaust"—the ultimate destruction by fire—Gatsby, too, perishes.

As in Donne's "Elegie XIX"—and, among twentieth-century authors, in Joyce's *Ulysses,* Eliot's *Prufrock, The Waste Land,* and *Four Quartets,* and Hart Crane's *The Bridge*—sexual union in *The Great Gatsby* serves partly as symbol of incarnation, that most basic union of spirit with matter. Donne writes "to his Mistris going to bed":

> Now off with those shooes, and then safely tread
> In this loves hallow'd temple, this soft bed.

In such white robes, heaven's Angels us'd to be
Receavd by men. . . .
O my America! my new-found-land,
My kingdome, safeliest when with one man man'd,
My Myne of precious stones, My Emperie,
How blest am I in this discovering thee! [27]

Though without Donne's irony, Fitzgerald writes:

[Gatsby's] heart beat faster and faster as Daisy's white face came up to his own. He knew that when he kissed this girl, and forever wed his unutterable visions to her perishable breath, his mind would never romp again like the mind of God. So he waited, listening for a moment longer to the tuning-fork that had been struck upon a star. Then he kissed her. At his lips' touch she blossomed for him like a flower and the incarnation was complete. (112)

Fitzgerald appropriates terminology from Christianity, but Gatsby entirely creates his own "religion." He makes his God a gigantic extension of his own "unutterable visions," then creates himself as a son of God:

The truth was that Jay Gatsby of West Egg, Long Island, sprang from his Platonic conception of himself. He was a son of God—a phrase which, if it means anything, means just that—and he must be about his Father's business, the service of a vast, vulgar, and meretricious beauty. So he invented just the sort of Jay Gatsby that a seventeen-year-old boy would be likely to invent, and to this conception he was faithful to the end. (99)

Fitzgerald subtly extends this religious motif through the novel, and it is perhaps not an extravagance to suggest that Daisy Fay becomes Gatsby's version of the Virgin Mary, both mother and bride of "God," that Gatsby founds his church (his absurd mansion) upon the rock of West Egg, and that the "vast, vulgar and meretricious beauty" composes his sacraments. This adds depth, for example, to Daisy's communion with Gatsby's shirts, "shirts of sheer linen and thick silk and fine flannel . . . the soft rich heap . . . shirts with stripes and scrolls and plaids in coral and apple-green and lavender and faint orange, with monograms of Indian blue.

Suddenly, with a strained sound, Daisy bent her head into the shirts and began to cry stormily.

---

[27] John Donne, *Complete Poems* (New York: Modern Library, 1952), p. 83. Cf. also Edwin Fussell, "Fitzgerald's Brave New World," *English Literary History*, XIX (Dec. 1952), 291-306.

"They're such beautiful shirts," she sobbed, her voice muffled in the thick folds. "It makes me sad because I've never seen such—such beautiful shirts before." (93-4)

But it is clear even from Fitzgerald's rhetoric that this "incarnation" is a fiction, that matter and flesh—"meretricious beauty" and Daisy Fay—are incompatible with Gatsby's spirit and that there is no union. As the "colossal significance" which Gatsby wills upon the green light at the end of Daisy's dock vanishes, so does the colossal significance of Daisy herself. (94) The sexual act becomes reduced to the bare physical event, nothing more. Untouched by the dream, Daisy remains part of a "secret society" with her brutal husband. (18) Her "voice full of money," (120) she belongs to the chaotic materialism which Gatsby strives unsuccessfully to order. In the end, she creates disorder:

It was all very careless and confused. They were careless people, Tom and Daisy—they smashed up things and creatures and then retreated back into their money or their vast carelessness, or whatever it was that kept them together, and let other people clean up the mess they had made. . . . (181)

"O my America! my new-found-land," Donne writes, describing his mistress at her moment of "full nakedness." On *Gatsby*'s final page, Fitzgerald reverses the metaphor: America at her moment of discovery becomes a woman; her discovery is the sexual union which symbolizes incarnation. America promises to be the terrestrial paradise, God's kingdom on earth, ordering spirit united with and uniting chaotic matter:

as the moon rose higher the inessential houses began to melt away until gradually I became aware of the old island here that flowered once for Dutch sailors' eyes—a fresh green breast of the new world. Its vanished trees, the trees that had made way for Gatsby's house, had once pandered in whispers to the last and greatest of all human dreams; for a transitory enchanted moment man must have held his breath in the presence of this continent, compelled into an aesthetic contemplation he neither understood nor desired, face to face for the last time in history with something commensurate to his capacity for wonder. (182)

Here again Fitzgerald's rhetoric undercuts at the very moment of affirmation. The "fresh green breast of the new world" "flowered" for the Dutch sailors just as Daisy "blossomed . . . like a flower" for Gatsby. The trees "pander": it is as if Donne's mistress becomes a whore, bought with money as Gatsby tried to buy Daisy. Looking back upon the novel, one sees how the Dutch settlers turned into Dan Cody, the "pioneer debauchee," the plunderer ("—Yet no delirium

of jewels! O Fernando," Hart Crane's returning Columbus had futilely
admonished his king. "Take of that eastern shore, this western sea, /
Yet yield thy God's, thy Virgin's charity! /—Rush down the plenitude,
and you shall see / Isaiah counting famine on this lee!" [28]). The very
name of Gatsby's first mentor, Dan Cody, implies this corruption;
Daniel Boone, the true pioneer, combines with William Cody, buf-
falo-slaughterer and carnival man. Corrupter of America, Cody is
"soft-minded," "a gray, florid man with a hard, empty face," possessed
of lust and greed; like Myrtle Wilson, he is flesh without spirit. (101)
Even if the new world was in fact "commensurate to [man's] capacity
for wonder"—nonhuman matter commensurate to the human spirit
—process immediately annulled this moment of union, thanks partly
to men like Cody. Such dreams of order appear doomed.

Yet man must persist in dreaming his fictions, the novel implies,
or go under. As Wallace Stevens has said, "the final belief is to believe
in a fiction, which you know to be a fiction, there being nothing else.
The exquisite truth is to know that it is a fiction and that you believe
in it willingly." [29] The statement applies with special force to *The
Great Gatsby*, where man must impose his fictions of order, meaning,
and permanence upon a multiverse in process, which, hostile or in-
different, nonhumanly rejects them. These "unreal" fictions are man's
only shield against destruction; they alone, paradoxically, are "real"
to man (100); Chaos, as in *The Waste Land*, is "unreal," and it is
through these fictions that man expresses his basic instinct for survival.
Man needs an "extra gardener" to impose order upon recalcitrant
nature. (39) Thus, in a "pointless" atmosphere of "broken fragments,"
Nick Carraway's "instinct [is] to telephone immediately for the
police"—invoking the human fiction of law and order. (16) Gatsby,
on the other hand, operates outside conventional standards of order;
"taking a white card from his wallet," he subverts the policeman's
function. (68) Here lies the deepest meaning of Gatsby's gangsterism;
instead of invoking conventional fictions like Nick ("the world . . .
in uni..orm and at . . . moral attention forever."), Gatsby creates his
own identity, his own God, his own private morality. Wholly existen-
tial, he creates an individual fiction without recourse to or comfort
from the "wise," and to this fiction he is "faithful to the end." As a
more recent novel puts it:

> [Man] is by mindless lust engendered and by mindless wrench ex-
> pelled, from the Eden of the womb to the motley, mindless world. He
> is Chance's fool, the toy of aimless Nature—a mayfly flitting down the
> winds of Chaos! . . .

[28] Hart Crane, *The Complete Poems*, ed. Waldo Frank (Garden City, N.Y., 1958),
p. 7.
[29] Wallace Stevens, "Adagia," *Opus Posthumous* (New York, 1957), p. 163.

One must needs make and seize his soul, and then cleave fast to't, or
go babbling in the corner; one must choose his gods and devils on the
run, quill his own name upon the universe, and declare, ' 'Tis *I*, and the
world stands such-a-way!' One must *assert, assert, assert,* or go screaming
mad. What other course remains? [30]

Nick affirms the value of Gatsby's failed dream, because Gatsby so
fully asserts human meaning against the "winds of chaos," while the
rest, except for Nick, become all but indistinguishable from it.
"They're a rotten crowd," Nick shouts to Gatsby. "You're worth the
whole damn bunch put together." (154)

The ultimate fiction in *The Great Gatsby,* of course, is not Gatsby's
dream. This fiction is the novel itself.[31] If the novel were exactly
mimetic of the world it portrays, the novel would *be* meaningless
chaos; instead, as Fitzgerald intended, *Gatsby* is "something new,
something extraordinary and beautiful and simple and intricately
patterned," [32] a work of art *eloquent of* chaos. Like the "colossal
vitality of [Gatsby's] illusion," the novel, into which Fitzgerald has
"thrown himself . . . with a creative passion," goes "beyond everything." (97) Fitzgerald explicitly indicates the selective patterning of
his art when he makes Nick write toward the end of Chapter III:

Reading over what I have written so far, I see I have given the impression that the events of three nights several weeks apart were all that
absorbed me. On the contrary, they were merely casual events in a
crowded summer, and, until much later, they absorbed me infinitely less
than my personal affairs. (56)

The novelist selects from indiscriminate process according to some
fictional pattern of his own which itself constitutes an act of selection
(a humorous example is Vladimir Tostoff's *Jazz History of the World,*
p. 50). Outside the realm of human fiction, the nature of things appears "accidental"; thus when Gatsby's dream dies and Gatsby's body
floats "irregularly" in the pool, Fitzgerald writes, "A small gust of
wind that scarcely corrugated the surface was enough to disturb its
accidental course with its *accidental* burden." (162, italics added)
Yet in a triumph of art, Fitzgerald makes even accidents seem unac-
cidental, incorporates "real" disorder within fictional order. He ac-
complishes this by repetition (in the "real" world, repetition does not
exist): the accident involving Tom and the chambermaid, the reference to both Nick and Jordan Baker as "bad drivers," the wreck just

[30] John Barth, *The Sot-Weed Factor* (New York, 1960), pp. 364-5.
[31] Cf. Robert Klawitter, "Henri Bergson and James Joyce's Fictional World,"
Comparative Literature Studies, III (1966), 429-437.
[32] Fitzgerald, letter to Maxwell Perkins, July, 1922, quoted in Kenneth Eble,
F. Scott Fitzgerald (New Haven, 1963), p. 88.

outside Gatsby's driveway after his party in which, as in Tom's accident, a wheel is ripped off, the hit-and-run death of Myrtle Wilson, and finally the accidental conjunction of events which leads to Gatsby's murder and Wilson's suicide. This is merely one of many patterns which dovetail in *The Great Gatsby*. The more significant of these are discussed in the following essays. It is enough to assert here that *The Great Gatsby* asserts the value of human order in defiance of all which defeats it. In Nick's words, the novel opens a "single window" on "the inexhaustible variety of life," a unified perspective on the condition of man in his multiverse.

Editor's Note

The seven longer essays in this volume speak for themselves. The standards governing their selection have been excellence and variety, and all rank among the best, most intelligent writing about *The Great Gatsby*.

The material in "Viewpoints"—beginning with Maxwell Perkins' criticism and praise of the original version of the novel, which Fitzgerald was to revise almost up to the day of publication, ending with Fitzgerald's tough, moving letter to his daughter—should give the reader a sense of the high value which major writers, critics, and Fitzgerald himself place upon the novel.

PART ONE

Interpretations

Boats Against the Current

by James E. Miller, Jr.

Shortly before publication of *The Great Gatsby,* Fitzgerald wrote to John Peale Bishop, "[one of the] cheerfulest things in my life [is] . . . the hope that my book has something extraordinary about it." [1] Although one reviewer thought that *The Great Gatsby* was "a book of the season only," [2] and another that it was "not a good book, but . . . superior to [Fitzgerald's] others with the exception of the first," [3] most reviewers agreed with Fitzgerald that there was something "extraordinary" about his novel. William Rose Benét's review summarized the extraordinary qualities: "The Great Gatsby reveals thoroughly matured craftsmanship. It has structure. It has high occasions of felicitous, almost magic, phrase. And most of all, it is out of the mirage. For the first time Fitzgerald surveys the Babylonian captivity of this era unblinded by the bright lights." [4] Almost every reviewer, like Benét, noted Fitzgerald's new moral perspective and skilled craftsmanship. Had Fitzgerald not matured in his attitude toward his material, his technique would have failed; had he not developed an "aesthetic ideal," his theme would have been obscured. Actually, Fitzgerald achieved so rare a balance among the many demanding requirements of fiction that, as one critic said, *The Great Gatsby* "is an almost perfectly fulfilled intention." [5]

Jay Gatsby is the most clearly projected of the tribe of Fitzgerald

---

"Boats Against the Current" by *James E. Miller, Jr.* From F. Scott Fitzgerald, His Art and His Technique (*New York: New York University Press, 1964*), *pp. 105-26.* Copyright © *1964 by New York University Press. Reprinted by permission of the publisher.*

[1] Fitzgerald, "Letters to Friends," *The Crack-Up* (New York: New Directions, 1945), p. 269.

[2] Isabel Paterson, "Up to the Minute," New York *Herald Tribune Books,* April 19, 1925, p. 6.

[3] "New Books in Brief Review," *The Independent,* CXIV (May 2, 1925), 507.

[4] William Rose Benét, "An Admirable Novel," *The Saturday Review of Literature,* I (May 9, 1925), 740.

[5] Paterson, "Up to the Minute," *op. cit.,* p. 6.

heroes who are in pursuit of an elusive dream which, even though
sometimes within their grasp, continues somehow to evade them.
What makes Gatsby tower over Amory Blaine, Dexter Green, and
George O'Kelly is the greater magnitude of his glittering illusion and
the single-mindedness with which he tries to make it a reality. In *The
Great Gatsby*, the disastrous events of the summer of 1922 which bring
to a close Gatsby's quest of the "grail" (179) [6] are related by Nick
Carraway. He is the witness of a series of bizarre scenes in which
Gatsby comes close to the attainment of Daisy Buchanan, personify-
ing the dazzling world of his vision, but fails when he is caught in the
backwash of the tawdry affair between Tom Buchanan and his mistress, Myrtle Wilson. Gatsby, unlike the other Fitzgerald heroes,
sacrifices his life on the altar of his dream, unaware that it is composed of the ephemeral stuff of the past.

In *The Great Gatsby*, Fitzgerald abandoned the omniscient point
of view he had previously used in his novels and resorted to first-person narration, after the manner of Joseph Conrad. Until Conrad's
special use of the first person, the method had been in disrepute
among writers who thought of fiction primarily in terms of technique.
Henry James, as Richard P. Blackmur has said, "bore a little heavily
against this most familiar of all narrative methods." [7] James thought
that the method led inevitably to irrelevance and saturation. In dis-
cussing the representation of Strether in *The Ambassadors*, James
remarked, "suffice it, to be brief, that the first person, in the long
piece, is a form foredoomed to looseness, and that looseness, never
much my affair, had never been so little so on this particular occasion." [8] Although James's comments on Strether are concerned with
the *first person* as hero, his points seem aimed against the method
generally. James had plenty of examples from literary history of
novels in the first person which were chronicles "foredoomed to looseness." *David Copperfield* is one that comes readily to mind; Willa
Cather's *My Ántonia* is a modern example of such a novel with
"variety . . . smuggled in by the back door."

But Conrad's use of the first person did not lead to the looseness
which James so much feared. In *The Nigger of the Narcissus* (1897),
Conrad began as the omniscient author but, after a few pages, shifted
to the first person, placing the narrator on board the ship among the
crew. The alternation between the first and third persons continued
throughout the novel, and, as Joseph Warren Beach says, "technically

[6] Quotations from *The Great Gatsby* (New York: Charles Scribner's Sons, 1925)
will be identified in the text by page numbers in parentheses.
[7] Richard P. Blackmur, "Introduction," *The Art of the Novel: Critical Prefaces*
(New York: Scribner's, 1947), by Henry James, p. xxix.
[8] James, *The Art of the Novel*, p. 320.

it appears as a kind of exercise in story-telling, *in the course of which* only [Conrad] stumbled upon methods which might come in as a supplement to the nice power of words." [9] Conrad exploited the "modified" first-person technique in a series of stories—"Youth," "Heart of Darkness," *Lord Jim,* and *Chance*—in which Marlow acts as narrator, but not in the conventional first-person manner. By the use of a series of technical devices, Conrad avoided the usual pitfalls and limitations of first-person narration.

In *Chance,* for example, the story is told by Marlow to "me," presumably the author, who appears very little except to ask questions now and then of the narrator. Marlow relates the story in the first person, but, when he finds that he cannot "reconstruct" an event (and he is allowed considerable liberties of imagination), he does not hesitate to quote extensively a character who possesses the particular knowledge that he desires. A character quoted by Marlow may in turn relay information from another character, so that the happening, by the time it reaches the reader, has in effect filtered through a number of minds. In this way Conrad makes the first-person narrative serve him as a flexible device in presenting a variety of points of view. But always there, relentlessly pursuing the "subject," is Marlow, who "hold[s] up unquestioningly . . . the rescued fragment" to search out "the substance of its truth."

In spite of his dislike for first-person narration because of its inevitable "looseness," Henry James, it will be recalled, cited Conrad's *Chance* as an example of the novel of selection. Conrad, James said, had multiplied "his creators or . . . producers, as to make them almost more numerous and quite emphatically more material than the creatures and the production itself." By placing the narrator in the story and letting him reconstruct and interpret, by turning over all of his "duties" as author to him, Conrad succeeded in effacing himself almost completely. The reader remains unconscious of the author behind the scenes but he becomes acutely conscious of the narrator as a character in the story.

Fitzgerald used the modified first-person in *The Great Gatsby* much as Conrad used it in the Marlow stories. Nick Carraway is charged with relating the story as he sees it, reconstructing by some means whatever he himself has been unable to witness. His qualification as a sympathetic listener is carefully established on the first page of the novel: "I'm inclined to reserve all judgments, a habit that has opened up many curious natures to me and also made me the victim of not a few veteran bores. . . ." Such a characteristic is mandatory for an

---

[9] Joseph Warren Beach, *The Twentieth Century Novel* (New York: Appleton-Century-Crofts, 1932), p. 349.

observer who must rely to a great extent on other people for information about those events which he himself is unable to witness.

There are three methods by which Nick Carraway informs the reader of what is happening or has happened in *The Great Gatsby:* most frequently he presents his own eye-witness account; often he presents the accounts of other people, sometimes in their words, sometimes in his own; occasionally he reconstructs an event from several sources—the newspapers, servants, his own imagination—but presents his version as connected narrative. Nick is initially placed at the edge of the story: he rents a cottage next to Gatsby's mansion in West Egg, and he is remotely related to the Buchanans (he is "second cousin once removed" to Daisy, and he was at Yale with her husband, Tom), who live across the bay in East Egg. This slight relationship is gradually strengthened, particularly through Jordan Baker, whom he meets at the Buchanans, until Nick becomes, in spite of his reluctance, involved in Gatsby's pursuit of Daisy, the material symbol of his dream. Nick's position becomes such that he is naturally able to witness and report personally a maximum of the "contemporary" action. Various devices are used to keep him on stage when Fitzgerald wishes to represent an event scenically through him. During the showdown scene between Tom and Gatsby, Nick informs the reader: "At this point [after it is apparent that an argument between Tom and Gatsby is developing] Jordan and I tried to go, but Tom and Gatsby insisted with competitive firmness that we remain—as though neither of them had anything to conceal and it would be a privilege to partake vicariously of their emotions" (157). Nick's presence is carefully justified in order to enable him to present an eye-witness account of this important incident.

When Fitzgerald needs to inform the reader of material about which his narrator can have no firsthand knowledge, he sometimes permits Nick to listen extensively to an individual who has the information. Jordan Baker, one of the most technically useful characters in the book (like a Henry James *ficelle,* however, she is also granted a dramatic interest in the story[10]), informs Nick of the brief wartime love affair between Daisy and Gatsby, which had taken place some five years before. Her eye-witness account begins:

[10] James, *The Art of the Novel,* p. 324: "To project imaginatively, for my hero, a relation [with a *ficelle*] that has nothing to do with the matter (the matter of my subject) but has everything to do with the manner (the manner of my presentation of the same) and yet to treat it, at close quarters and for fully economic expression's possible sake, as if it were important and essential—to do that sort of thing and yet muddle nothing may easily become, as one goes, a signally attaching proposition. . . ." Fitzgerald, it seems, has met and overcome this "signally attaching proposition" admirably: Jordan Baker, who belongs more to the treatment than to the subject, is yet given a well-defined character and a significant role in the action.

One October day in nineteen-seventeen—
(said Jordan Baker that afternoon, sitting up very straight on a straight chair in the tea-garden at the Plaza Hotel)
—I was walking along from one place to another, half on the sidewalks and half on the lawns (89).

By this simple device, a past event is represented fully from a point of view other than the narrator's.

Sometimes Fitzgerald permits his narrator to reconstruct in his own language what he has been told about some event he has not witnessed. Citing Gatsby as his source, Nick informs the reader of Gatsby's days with Dan Cody: "James Gatz—that was really, or at least legally, his name. He had changed it at the age of seventeen and at the specific moment that witnessed the beginning of his career —when he saw Dan Cody's yacht drop anchor over the most insidious flat on Lake Superior" (118). This method permits Nick to intersperse speculation and interpretation with the action: "The truth was that Jay Gatsby of West Egg, Long Island, sprang from his Platonic conception of himself. He was a son of God—a phrase which, if it means anything, means just that—and he must be about his Father's business, the service of a vast, vulgar, and meretricious beauty" (118). Had he simply "overheard" Gatsby telling the story of his youth, the reader would have been deprived of Nick's imaginative conception of Gatsby's past.

In order to present as dramatically and connectedly as possible a scene at which there is no surviving observer, Fitzgerald occasionally allows the narrator to reconstruct an event rather freely from several sources, unstated but implied. In such a manner Nick describes the day on which Wilson tracks down and shoots Gatsby and then kills himself. Nick begins by saying, "Now I want to go back a little and tell what happened at the garage after we left there the night before" (187). There follows a dramatic representation of Wilson's eccentric behavior, which Nick could have pieced together only from an account by Wilson's sole companion, Michaelis, who runs a coffee shop near the Wilson garage. But when Wilson sets out alone in the early morning on his mission of death, Nick's source of information becomes the newspapers or testimony at the inquest: "His movements—he was on foot all the time—were afterward traced to Port Roosevelt and then Gad's Hill, where he bought a sandwich that he didn't eat, and a cup of coffee. . . . By half-past two he was in West Egg, where he asked some one the way to Gatsby's house. So by that time he knew Gatsby's name" (192-93). Nick shifts next to an account of Gatsby's actions at about this time: "At two o'clock Gatsby put on his bathing-suit and left word with the butler that if anyone phoned word was to be

brought to him at the pool" (193). At this point and later in his account, Nick reconstructs Gatsby's actions from various servants—the
butler, the chauffeur, and the gardener. But once Gatsby is alone,
Nick's only resource is his imagination: "He must have looked up at
an unfamiliar sky through frightening leaves and shivered as he found
what a grotesque thing a rose is and how raw the sunlight was upon
the scarcely created grass. A new world, material without being real,
where poor ghosts, breathing dreams like air, drifted fortuitously
about . . . like that ashen, fantastic figure gliding toward him
through the amorphous trees" (194). This entire series of events is
pieced together in proper order, placed in perspective, and presented
by Nick as connected narrative. Whatever deficiences in knowledge
Nick has are made up for amply by his fertile imagination.

Fitzgerald's use of the modified first-person enables him to avoid
"the large false face peering around the corner of a character's
head." [11] By giving Nick logical connections with the people he is
observing, by always making his presence or absence at the events
probable, not accidental, and by allowing him several natural sources
of information which he may use freely, Fitzgerald achieves a realism
impossible to an "omniscient" author or even to a limited third-per-
son point of view: through Nick Carraway, Fitzgerald places the
reader in direct touch with the action, eliminating himself, as author,
entirely. What Fitzgerald says of Cecilia, in his notes to *The Last
Tycoon,* might well apply to Nick in *The Great Gatsby:* "by making
Cecilia, at the moment of her telling the story, an intelligent and ob-
servant woman, I shall grant myself the privilege, as Conrad did, of
letting her imagine the actions of the characters. Thus, I hope to get
the verisimilitude of a first person narrative, combined with a God-
like knowledge of all events that happen to my characters." [12] Fitzgerald could have substituted his own name for Conrad's had he
recalled Nick Carraway. *The Great Gatsby* is a minor masterpiece
illustrating beautifully Conrad's governing literary intent "to make
you *see.*"

The manner of the representation of events in *The Great Gatsby,*
especially the order in which they are related, seems to follow a pattern derived (in part) also from Conrad. Ford Madox Ford, who col-
laborated with Conrad on a number of early novels, explained the
theory behind the reordering of events to create a deliberate "confusion":

[11] Fitzgerald, "Introduction," *The Great Gatsby* (New York: Modern Library,
1934), p. x.
[12] Fitzgerald, *The Last Tycoon* (New York: Charles Scribner's Sons, 1941), pp. 139-
40.

It became very early evident to us that what was the matter with the novel, and the British novel in particular, was that it went straight forward, whereas in your gradual making acquaintanceship with your fellows you never do go straight forward. You meet an English gentleman at your golf club. He is beefy, full of health, the moral of the boy from an English Public School of the finest type. You discover gradually that he is hopelessly neurasthenic, dishonest in matters of small change, but unexpectedly self-sacrificing, a dreadful liar. . . . To get such a man in fiction you could not begin at his beginning and work his life chronologically to the end. You must first get him in with a strong impression, and then work backwards and forwards over his past. . . . That theory at least we gradually evolved.[13]

In real life, the story of an acquaintance comes into focus only after apparently unrelated incidents from different periods of time are gradually pieced together; and, unless the individual makes "a strong impression" in the beginning, there is little incentive for one to go to the trouble of discovering the incidents of his life. A story told in this manner gains not only in verisimilitude, however, but also in suspense: pieces of the protagonist's life can be so arranged and revealed as to create mystery, which is particularly effective if there is a sensitive observer to share the reader's bewilderment.

One of the best examples of Conrad's use of this device occurs in *Lord Jim*. Joseph Warren Beach has plotted graphically Conrad's rearrangement of the chronology in this novel: "The true chronological order would be:

A,B,C,D,E,F,G,H,I,J,K,L,M,N,O,P,Q,R,S,T,U,V,W,X,Y,Z

The order in the book is, by chapters:

KLMP, WA, E, B, E, E, H, GD, HJ, FE, E, E, F, F, F, FK, I, I, R, I, KL, MN, N, Q, QPO, OP, P, QP, P, P, P, QP, P, P, Q, Q, Q, R, ZV, XY, S, S, S, TY, U, U, U, WXY"[14]

This hopelessly scrambled alphabet shows to just what extent Conrad did depart from the traditional "straight forward" method of the British novel. An undated passage in Fitzgerald's notebooks suggests that he was aware of Conrad's method and its purpose: "Conrad's secret theory examined: He knew that things do transpire about people. Therefore he wrote the truth and transposed it to parallel to give that quality, adding confusion however to his structure. Nevertheless,

---

[13] Ford Madox Ford, *Joseph Conrad: A Personal Remembrance* (Boston: Little, Brown, 1924), pp. 136-37.

[14] Beach, *The Twentieth-Century Novel*, p. 363.

there is in his scheme a desire to imitate life which is in all the big shots." [15] Although this remark might well have been jotted down some time after 1925, Fitzgerald was probably, consciously or unconsciously, following Conrad's method in *The Great Gatsby.*

Fitzgerald does, certainly, get Gatsby in first with a strong impression. When, at the opening of the novel, Nick goes over to the Buchanans for dinner, all he knows about Gatsby is that a man by that name inhabits the fabulous mansion to the right of his cottage. During the course of the evening, Jordan Baker asks Nick if he knows Gatsby, and Nick feels that this "would do for an introduction" (26) when, later that evening after he has returned home, he sees Gatsby standing out on his lawn: "But I didn't call to him, for he gave a sudden intimation that he was content to be alone—he stretched out his arms toward the dark water in a curious way, and, far as I was from him, I could have sworn he was trembling. Involuntarily I glanced seaward—and distinguished nothing except a single green light, minute and far away, that might have been the end of a dock. When I looked once more for Gatsby he had vanished, and I was alone again in the unquiet darkness" (26). After this brief but dramatically impressive first glimpse of Gatsby, Fitzgerald works "backwards and forwards" over his past until the complete portrait finally emerges at the end of the book. Just how much Fitzgerald has rearranged the events of Gatsby's life can be seen by tracing events through the book chronologically; the only glimpse of Gatsby's boyhood is in the last chapter; the account of Gatsby, at the age of seventeen, joining Dan Cody's yacht comes in Chapter VI; the important love affair between Gatsby and Daisy, which took place five years before the action in the book when Gatsby, then in the army, first met Daisy, is related three separate times (Chapters IV, VI, and VIII), but from various points of view and with various degrees of fullness; the account of Gatsby's war experiences and his trip, after discharge, back to Louisville to Daisy's home, is given in Chapter VIII; and Gatsby's entry into his present mysterious occupation through Wolfsheim is presented, briefly, in Chapter IX. The summer of 1922, the last summer of Gatsby's life, acts as a string on to which these varicolored "beads" of his past have been "haphazardly" strung.

A simple diagram of the sequence of events in *The Great Gatsby* is, perhaps, helpful. Allowing X to stand for the straight chronological account of the summer of 1922, and A, B, C, D, and E to represent the significant events of Gatsby's past, the nine chapters of *The Great Gatsby* may be charted: X, X, X, XCX, X, XBXCX, X, XCXDX, XEXAX.

---

[15] Fitzgerald, "The Note-Books," *The Crack-Up,* p. 179.

Although Gatsby's life is gradually revealed in the novel as an acquaintance's life would probably emerge in real life, there is an artistic order in the disorder. In Nick's pursuit of the "substance of truth" in Gatsby's story, he passes on the information in the order in which he receives it—with one major exception. After briefly recounting Gatsby's days with Dan Cody, he adds: "[Gatsby] told me all this very much later, but I've put it down here with the idea of exploding those first wild rumors about his antecedents, which weren't even faintly true. Moreover he told it to me at a time of confusion, when I had reached the point of believing everything and nothing about him. So I take advantage of this short halt, while Gatsby, so to speak, caught his breath, to clear this set of misconceptions away" (122). Dozens of legends have accumulated around Gatsby: that he is a cousin of Kaiser Wilhelm, that he killed a man once, that he was a German spy, that he was an Oxford man, that he was involved in the "underground pipeline to Canada" (117), and even "that he didn't live in a house at all, but in a boat that looked like a house and was moved secretly up and down the Long Island shore" (117). A desirable amount of bewilderment, confusion, mystery, and suspense is created by these wild stories, but it is necessary that they gradually give way to something really as awe inspiring as the myths themselves, Gatsby's enormously vital illusion. And to understand that illusion, it is necessary to understand its origins, which go far deeper than the love for Daisy. Just as the first half of the novel is devoted to the inflation of the myth of Gatsby to gigantic proportions to give apparent support to the "colossal vitality of his illusion" (116), so the second half gradually deflates this myth through the revelation of the deepness of the roots of Gatsby's dream in the deprivations of his past. The one instance, mid-point in the novel, of Nick's departure from his method of conveying information as it is revealed to him is the book's "fulcrum": the legends must be cleared away so that there might be room for the truth to emerge.

Fitzgerald once remarked of *The Great Gatsby*, "What I cut out of it both physically and emotionally would make another novel." [16] This confession reveals something of the "selective delicacy" with which he dealt with his material. In *The Great Gatsby*, as in neither of his previous novels, the "subject" is unfailingly and remorselessly pursued from beginning to end; yet, contrary to Wells, this novel gives the impression of being more "like life" than either of the other two. Fitzgerald's sympathetic observer, who is narrating the story in retrospect, provides a natural selection, as does the limiting of the action to one summer. But even within these restrictions, Fitzgerald could have

---

[16] Fitzgerald, "Introduction," *The Great Gatsby*, p. x.

indulged in irrelevance or expansiveness. And as a matter of fact, a number of his literary peers criticized *The Great Gatsby* because of its *slightness*. Edith Wharton wrote: "My present quarrel with you is only this: that to make Gatsby really Great, you ought to have given us his early career (not from the cradle—but from his visit to the yacht, if not before) instead of a short resumé of it. That would have situated him, & made his final tragedy a tragedy instead of a 'fait divers' for the morning papers." [17] Fitzgerald wrote to John Peale Bishop about his criticism of *The Great Gatsby*, "It is about the only criticism that the book has had which has been intelligible, save a letter from Mrs. Wharton. . . . Also you are right about Gatsby being blurred and patchy." [18]

Fitzgerald had, of course, experimented with and discarded a prologue to *The Great Gatsby* ("Absolution"), which would have revealed much of Gatsby's origin and boyhood. It is a delicate critical problem to determine just how much of Gatsby's past should have been included in the novel. There seems no doubt that Fitzgerald has selected for representation those events of the past which are keys to Gatsby's character and dream. The blurring of Gatsby, if it is a defect, is also a virtue, in that it renders his fantastic illusion more believable.

One of the most effective devices of selection which Fitzgerald employed, enabling him to create the illusion of comprehensiveness and completeness without an actual excess of detail, is the list of names of those who attended Gatsby's parties that fateful summer. Nick tells the reader:

> Once I wrote down on the empty spaces of a time-table the names of those who came to Gatsby's house that summer. It is an old time-table now, disintegrating at its folds, and headed "This schedule in effect July 5th, 1922." But I can still read the gray names, and they will give you a better impression than my generalities of those who accepted Gatsby's hospitality and paid him the subtle tribute of knowing nothing whatever about him.
>
> From East Egg, then, came the Chester Beckers and the Leeches, and a man named Bunsen, whom I knew at Yale, and Doctor Webster Civit, who was drowned last summer up in Maine. And the Hornbeams and the Willie Voltaires, and a whole clan named Blackbuck, who always gathered in a corner and flipped up their noses like goats at whosoever came near. And the Ismays and the Chrysties (or rather Hubert Auerbach and Mr. Chrystie's wife), and Edgar Beaver, whose hair, they say, turned cotton-white one winter afternoon for no good reason at all (73-74).

[17] Edith Wharton, one of "Three Letters about 'The Great Gatsby,' " *The Crack-Up*, p. 309.

[18] Fitzgerald, "Letters to Friends," *The Crack-Up*, p. 271.

The list continues for some two pages, imaginatively evoking a series of fabulous parties attended by an endless number of people—colorful, eccentric, fashionable, ambitious, bored—people, who, although they do not know Gatsby, take advantage of the opportunity to drink his liquor and eat his food. Aside from the intrinsic value as superb satire, the device (compare the enumeration of Gloria's suitors in *The Beautiful and Damned*, pp. 144-45) gives the impression, in a very short space and with a minimum of detail, of a continuous round of parties at Gatsby's place—an impression which prevents from seeming arbitrarily selective the scenic presentation of the two parties concerned directly with the "subject."

The Great Gatsby is constructed as a series of scenes dramatizing the important events of the story and connected by brief passages of interpretation and summary. The first three chapters of the book, for example, are devoted to the preparation for and presentation of three scenes: the comparatively "proper" dinner party at the Buchanan's in East Egg, the wild drunken party at Tom and Myrtle's apartment in New York, and the huge, extravagant party at Gatsby's mansion in West Egg. These scenes serve to introduce, dramatically, all of the important characters and places in the novel and seem, perhaps, so selective as to give the impression of artificiality. As though aware of this possibility, Nick confides to the reader at the end of the third scene:

> Reading over what I have written so far, I see I have given the impression that the events of three nights several weeks apart were all that absorbed me. On the contrary, they were merely casual events in a crowded summer, and, until much later, they absorbed me infinitely less than my personal affairs.
>
> Most of the time I worked. In the early morning the sun threw my shadow westward as I hurried down the white chasms of lower New York to the Probity Trust (68).

This summary of Nick's more or less routine life, which consumes some three or four pages, gives a realistic touch to the book without weighting it with unnecessary and irrelevant detail. Fitzgerald's sure touch in selecting the relevant events for dramatic representation, and for relegating the only obliquely related incidents to summary treatment or panoramic narration, enables him not only to sustain a compelling verisimilitude but also to avoid the "looseness" which Henry James thought inevitable in first-person narration.

In "The Rich Boy," Fitzgerald suggested the manner in which he had achieved objectivity—the way in which he had kept himself from being blinded by the glittering shimmer of superficial sophistication: "Let me tell you about the very rich. They are different from you and me. They possess and enjoy early, and it does something to them, makes them soft where we are hard, and cynical where we are trustful, in a way that, unless you were born rich, it is very difficult to understand. . . . They are different. The only way I can describe young Anson Hunter [the protagonist] is to approach him as if he were a foreigner and cling stubbornly to my point of view. If I accept his for a moment I am lost—I have nothing to show but a preposterous movie." [19] Too often in his previous novels and stories, Fitzgerald had been unable to differentiate between his own and the points of view of his fabulous characters, and too often he had ended with nothing but a "preposterous" scenario. In *The Great Gatsby,* as in "The Rich Boy" written immediately after, Fitzgerald clung stubbornly to his point of view, the mature view of a disinterested observer gifted with an acute sense of the "fundamental decencies."

Fitzgerald fulfills the obligation imposed by the device of the sensitive observer; he must make *The Great Gatsby* in some sense the observer's story, and this he does by portraying Nick Carraway's gradual penetration to the corruption at the heart of the fabulous life of the rich Tom and Daisy Buchanan and, simultaneously, his gradual discovery of the fundamental innocence and the measureless vitality of Gatsby's dream. While Nick Carraway is narrating this change, a major modification of his initial judgments, he is guiding the reader to a similar moral evaluation of the characters. In the opening pages of the book, Fitzgerald establishes his narrator's moral position. Nick Carraway is, on the advice of his father, "inclined to reserve all judgments" (1) because he knows that "a sense of the fundamental decencies is parcelled out unequally at birth" (2). But his tolerance has a limit: "Conduct may be founded on the hard rock or the wet marshes, but after a certain point I don't care what it's founded on. When I came back from the East last autumn I felt that I wanted the world to be in uniform and at a sort of moral attention forever; I wanted no more riotous excursions with privileged glimpses into the human heart" (2). With Nick Carraway's attitude precisely established at the opening of the story, there can be no ambiguity, as there had been in Fitzgerald's previous novels, regarding the moral quality of his characters or the moral significance of their actions.

In one sense, the moral conflict in the novel is resolved into a conflict between East and West—the ancient and corrupt East and the raw but virtuous West. Nick Carraway attributes his moral attitude to his Middle Western background. At the end of the story, he asserts, "I see now that this has been a story of the West, after all—Tom and Gatsby, Daisy and Jordan and I, were all Westerners, and perhaps we possessed some deficiency in common which made us subtly unadapta-

---

[19] Fitzgerald, *All the Sad Young Men* (New York: Scribner's, 1926), pp. 1-2.

ble to Eastern life" (212). It is perhaps subtly significant that Tom and Daisy live in *East* Egg, since they are really better adapted to Eastern life than Nick and Gatsby, who live in *West* Egg. Perhaps Fitzgerald in dramatizing the conflict of East and West was remembering Edmund Wilson's advice: "it seems to me a great pity that [Fitzgerald] has not written more of the west; it is perhaps the only milieu that he thoroughly understands; when he approaches the east, he brings to it the standards of the wealthy west—the preoccupation with display, the love of magnificence and jazz, the vigorous social atmosphere of amiable flappers and youths comparatively unpoisoned as yet by the snobbery of the east." [20] Nick's experience in the East results in his return with relief to the West: "After Gatsby's death the East was haunted for me like that [a night scene by El Greco], distorted beyond my eyes' power of correction. So when the blue smoke of brittle leaves was in the air and the wind blew the wet laundry stiff on the line I decided to come back home" (213). "Back home," it seems clear, is a place where the fundamental decencies are observed and virtue is honored.

Tom and Daisy Buchanan represent the world of sophistication which had heretofore, by the sheer brightness of its glamour, blinded Fitzgerald to its frequent lack of a sense of those "fundamental decencies." Racial prejudice, when mouthed by Maury Noble in *The Beautiful and Damned,* had seemed smart philosophizing, even an important idea; when Tom Buchanan says, "It's up to us, who are the dominant race, to watch out or these other races will have control of things" (16), Nick Carraway sees that "something was making [Tom] nibble at the edge of stale ideas as if his sturdy physical egotism no longer nourished his peremptory heart" (25). When Gloria (in *The Beautiful and Damned*) had asserted her "fundamental sophistication" by her willingness to sacrifice everyone and everything for her own petty pleasure, she had been admired by the other characters and also, the reader felt, by the author; when Daisy Buchanan exclaims, "Sophisticated—God, I'm sophisticated," Nick Carraway feels the "basic insincerity" (21) of what she says. Upon meeting Tom accidentally after the death of Gatsby, Nick confesses:

> I couldn't forgive him or like him, but I saw that what he had done was, to him, entirely justified. It was all very careless and confused. They were careless people, Tom and Daisy—they smashed up things and creatures and then retreated back into their money or their vast carelessness, or whatever it was that kept them together, and let other people clean up the mess they had made. . . .
>
> I shook hands with him; it seemed silly not to, for I felt suddenly as

[20] Edmund Wilson, "The Literary Spotlight: F. Scott Fitzgerald," *The Bookman,* LV (March, 1922), 22.

though I were talking to a child. Then he went into the jewelry store to buy a pearl necklace—or perhaps only a pair of cuff buttons—rid of my provincial squeamishness forever (216).

Daisy and Tom, in spite of the bright gleam of their wealth and the immensely bored sophistication of their careless lives, are seen for what they are—as the "foul dust that floated in the wake" (3) of Gatsby's dreams.

It was only by struggling his way through to an objective view of his material that Fitzgerald was enabled to develop his theme as lucidly and emphatically as he did. In *This Side of Paradise,* Rosalind's glamour had blinded both Amory and the author. In "Winter Dreams," Dexter Green's illusion had failed to become more than his own private possession. In "The Sensible Thing," George O'Kelly's sense of loss had seemed no more than the nostalgic remembrance of puppy love. But in *The Great Gatsby,* Fitzgerald for the first time embodied his experience in a story which is not only realistically convincing but also invested with a meaning beyond the literal. One reviewer defined the theme of *The Great Gatsby* as that "of a soiled or rather cheap personality transfigured and rendered pathetically appealing through the possession of a passionate idealism." [21] Another reviewer described the book as "a superb impressionistic painting, vivid in colour, and sparkling with meaning." [22] Almost as vague as the previous definition is specific, these remarks do no more than hint at what the novel is about.

Shortly after publication of his novel, Fitzgerald wrote to Edmund Wilson, "of all the reviews [of *The Great Gatsby*], even the most enthusiastic, not one had the slightest idea what the book was about." [23] The meaning of the novel is presumably, neither obvious nor to be comprehended in a simple statement. In one sense, certainly, the theme is the potential tragedy of passionately idealizing an unworthy and even sinister object. But this narrow definition does not suggest the subtlety and complexity of meaning brilliantly achieved by the symbolism, by the imagery, and by the language itself; and it is in these elements that the book is "sparkling with meaning." This phrase recalls Conrad's "magic suggestiveness," and it seems likely that Fitzgerald was attempting to accomplish with language what Conrad had outlined in his preface to *The Nigger of the Narcissus:* "And it is only through complete, unswerving devotion to the perfect blending of form and substance; it is only through an unremitting never-discouraged care for the shape and

[21] Van Vechten, "Fitzgerald on the March," *The Nation,* CXX (May 20, 1925), 576.
[22] George Seldes, "Spring Flight," *The Dial,* LXXIX (August, 1925), 164.
[23] Fitzgerald, "Letters to Friends," *The Crack-Up,* p. 270.

ring of sentences that an approach can be made to plasticity, to colour, and that the light of magic suggestiveness may be brought to play for an evanescent instant over the commonplace surface of words: of the old, old words, worn thin, defaced by ages of careless usage." [24] Not only has Fitzgerald confessed that he had the words of Conrad's preface fresh in his mind when he set about to write *The Great Gatsby,* but he implied an understanding of Conrad's special use of language to define themes when, in May, 1923, he began a book review with a quotation from Conrad's "Youth": "I did not know how good a man I was till then. . . . I remember my youth and the feeling that will never come back any more—the feeling that I could last forever, outlast the sea, the earth, and all men, . . . the triumphant conviction of strength, the beat of life in the handful of dust, the glow in the heart that with every year grows dim, grows cold, grows small, and expires too soon—before life itself." [25] On the poetically rhythmical style of "Youth," Fitzgerald commented, "since that story I have found in nothing else even the echo of that lift and ring." This phrase, close to Conrad's own "shape and ring," suggests that Fitzgerald was fully aware of Conrad's theory of the use of language to extend meaning and, moreover, that he was probably attempting to follow in his own work Conrad's high, austere principles.

The closing lines of *The Great Gatsby* do echo the "lift and ring" of the passage Fitzgerald quoted from "Youth," and show how well Fitzgerald had mastered Conrad's art of magic suggestiveness:

> Most of the big shore places were closed now and there were hardly any lights except the shadowy, moving glow of a ferryboat across the Sound. And as the moon rose higher the inessential houses began to melt away until gradually I became aware of the old island here that flowered once for Dutch sailors' eyes—a fresh, green breast of the new world. Its vanished trees, the trees that had made way for Gatsby's house, had once pandered in whispers to the last and greatest of all human dreams; for a transitory enchanted moment man must have held his breath in the presence of this continent, compelled into an aesthetic contemplation he neither understood nor desired, face to face for the last time in history with something commensurate to his capacity for wonder.
>
> And as I sat there brooding on the old, unknown world, I thought of Gatsby's wonder when he first picked out the green light at the end of Daisy's dock. He had come a long way to this blue lawn, and his dream must have seemed so close that he could hardly fail to grasp it. He did

[24] Conrad, *The Nigger of the Narcissus* (New York: Doubleday, 1935), p. xiii.
[25] Fitzgerald, "Under Fire," *The Literary Review* of the New York *Evening Post,* May 26, 1923, p. 715.

not know that it was already behind him, somewhere back in that vast
obscurity beyond the city, where the dark fields of the republic rolled on
under the night.

Gatsby believed in the green light, the orgastic future that year by year
recedes before us. It eluded us then, but that's no matter—to-morrow
we will run faster, stretch out our arms farther. . . . And one fine morning—

So we beat on, boats against the current, borne back ceaselessly into the
past (217-18).

This passage—a "perfect blending of form and substance"—becomes more and more rhythmical simultaneously with the gradual
expansion of the significance of Gatsby's dream. There is first the iden-
tification of his dream with the dream of those who discovered and
settled the American continent—the "last and greatest of all human
dreams"; there is next the association of Gatsby's dream with the
dream of Modern America, lost somewhere in the "vast obscurity" of
the "dark fields of the republic"; there is finally the poignant
realization that all of these dreams are one and inseparable and
forever without our grasp, not because of a failure of will or effort
but rather because the dream is in reality a vision of the receding
and irrecoverable past. Nick Carraway's discovery is close to Marlow's
knowledge in "Youth": they both sense "a feeling that will never come
back any more," they both watch with an acute sense of tragedy "the
glow in the heart" grow dim. At the end of *My Ántonia* Jim Burden
could assert that he and Ántonia "possessed" the "precious, the incommunicable past"; the very fact that he felt the compulsion to
commit that past to a written record suggests that he felt insecure
in its possession. It was Nick's discovery that the past cannot be
"possessed"; he had watched Gatsby searching for a past (a "past"
that had not even had a momentary existence, that was the invention
of his imagination) and, ultimately, finding death in its stead.

The green light at the end of Buchanan's dock will draw us on
forever—but we shall never possess our Daisy, for she is a vision
that really doesn't exist. Nick Carraway sees the green light when he
catches his first brief glimpse of his neighbor; he sees Gatsby standing on his lawn, stretching his arms toward the dark water that sep-
arates East Egg from West Egg—Daisy from himself. When Nick looks
out across the water, there is nothing visible "except a single green
light, minute and far away, that might have been the end of a dock"
(26). The green light, the contemporary signal which peremptorily
summons the traveler on his way, serves well as the symbol for man
in hurried pursuit of a beckoning but ever-elusive dream. And, if
Gatsby's dream has particular application to America, as Lionel

Trilling has suggested, probably no better symbol than the green light could be used for America's restless, reckless pursuit of the "American Dream." [26]

There is one set of symbols that pervades the entire book and makes it, perhaps, a sharper commentary on contemporary civilization than the simple story would at first seem to provide. The symbols exist materially in a "certain desolate area of land" between West Egg and New York, near the Wilson garage:

> This is a valley of ashes—a fantastic farm where ashes grow like wheat into ridges and hills and grotesque gardens; where ashes take the forms of houses and chimneys and rising smoke and, finally, with a transcendent effort, of ash-gray men, who move dimly and already crumbling through the powdery air. Occasionally a line of gray cars crawls along an invisible track, gives out a ghastly creak, and comes to rest, and immediately the ash-gray men swarm up with leaden spades and stir up an impenetrable cloud, which screens their obscure operations from your sight.
>
> But above the gray land and the spasms of bleak dust which drift endlessly over it, you perceive, after a moment, the eyes of Doctor T. J. Eckleburg. The eyes of Doctor T. J. Eckleburg are blue and gigantic—their retinas are one yard high. They look out of no face, but, instead, from a pair of enormous yellow spectacles which pass over a non-existent nose. Evidently some wild wag of an oculist set them there to fatten his practice in the borough of Queens, and then sank down himself into eternal blindness, or forgot them and moved away. But his eyes, dimmed a little by many paintless days, under sun and rain, brood on over the solemn dumping ground (27-28).

On one level, certainly, the valley of ashes represents the gray, dismal environment of the Wilsons and the life of the class to which they belong. Standing at the edge of the Wilson property, the valley casts its white ashen dust over them and over all who stop at the garage. But, as Fitzgerald returns to the valley of ashes again and again and as he draws his characters one by one along the highway by its "spasms of bleak dust," the desolate area begins to take on a greater significance: it becomes the primary backdrop against which the tragedy is played out. At one point, Fitzgerald refers to the valley as "the waste land" (29), suggesting that it stands as a symbol for the spiritual aridity of the civilization about which he writes—the kind of barren and waterless land that T. S. Eliot had conceived in his poem of that name.

The gigantic eyes of Doctor T. J. Eckleburg, which "brood on

[26] Lionel Trilling, "Introduction," *The Great Gatsby* (New York: New Directions, 1945), p. viii.

over the solemn dumping ground," also take on greater meaning along with the valley of ashes. When Wilson, after his wife's death, informs Michaelis of his earlier suspicions of her, he gazes out the window:

> Wilson's glazed eyes turned out to the ash heaps, where small gray clouds took on fantastic shapes and scurried here and there in the faint dawn wind.
>
> "I spoke to her," he muttered, after a long silence. "I told her she might fool me but she couldn't fool God. I took her to the window"—with an effort he got up and walked to the rear window and leaned with his face pressed against it—"and I said 'God knows what you've been doing, everything you've been doing. You may fool me, but you can't fool God!' "
>
> Standing behind him, Michaelis saw with a shock that he was looking at the eyes of Doctor T. J. Eckleburg, which had just emerged, pale and enormous, from the dissolving night.
>
> "God sees everything," repeated Wilson.
>
> "That's an advertisement," Michaelis assured him. Something made him turn away from the window and look back into the room. But Wilson stood there a long time, his face close to the window pane, nodding into the twilight (191-92).

Just as Wilson comes half-consciously to identify the eyes of Doctor T. J. Eckleburg with God, so the reader gradually becomes aware of them as representing some kind of detached intellect, brooding gloomily over life in the bleak waste land surrounding it, and presiding fatalistically over the little tragedy enacted as if in sacrifice before it.

It is probably because these and other symbols "suggest" rather than "mean" that *The Great Gatsby* survives many readings and that with each reading it continues to "sparkle with meaning." The charming but sinister world of sophistication represented by Daisy and Tom, the world of illusion and dreams represented by Gatsby and the world of bleakness and ashen dust represented by the Wilsons converge and collide catastrophically to create not only a fascinating tale but also a fable filled with "magic suggestiveness." When in 1934, Fitzgerald reread *The Great Gatsby,* he did not feel "guilty of any discrepancy from the truth . . . truth or rather the equivalent of the truth, the attempt at honesty of imagination." [27] It is because of Fitzgerald's imaginative adherence to the truth, or its equivalent, in *The Great Gatsby* that the book, so much a book of its era, detaches itself from its period to have meaning and significance for a later day.

---

[27] F. Scott Fitzgerald, "Introduction," *The Great Gatsby*, p. x.

Scott Fitzgerald's Criticism
of America

by Marius Bewley

Critics of Scott Fitzgerald tend to agree that *The Great Gatsby* is somehow a commentary on that elusive phrase, the American dream. The assumption seems to be that Fitzgerald approved. On the contrary, it can be shown that *The Great Gatsby* offers some of the severest and closest criticism of the American dream that our literature affords. Read in this way, Fitzgerald's masterpiece ceases to be a pastoral documentary of the Jazz Age and takes its distinguished place among those great national novels whose profound corrective insights into the nature of American experience are not separable from the artistic form of the novel itself. That is to say, Fitzgerald—at least in this one book —is in a line with the greatest masters of American prose. *The Great Gatsby* embodies a criticism of American experience—not of manners, but of a basic historic attitude to life—more radical than anything in James's own assessment of the deficiencies of his country. The theme of *Gatsby* is the withering of the American dream.

Essentially, this phrase represents the romantic enlargement of the possibilities of life on a level at which the material and the spiritual have become inextricably confused. As such, it led inevitably toward the problem that has always confronted American artists dealing with American experience—the problem of determining the hidden boundary in the American vision of life at which the reality ends and the illusion begins. Historically, the American dream is anti-Calvinistic, and believes in the goodness of nature and man. It is accordingly a product of the frontier and the West rather than of the Puritan Tradition. The simultaneous operation of two such attitudes in American life created a tension out of which much of our greatest art has

"Scott Fitzgerald's Criticism of America" by *Marius Bewley. From* The Sewanee Review, *LXII (Spring, 1954), 223-46. Copyright © 1954 by The University of the South. This essay appeared in an expanded form in* The Eccentric Design: Form in the Classical American 'Novel *(New York: Columbia University Press, 1959; London: Chatto & Windus, Ltd., 1959). Reprinted by permission of* The Sewanee Review *and the author.*

sprung. Youth of the spirit—perhaps of the body as well—is a require-
ment of its existence; limit and deprivation are its blackest devils. But
it shows an astonishing incapacity to believe in them:

> I join you . . . in branding as cowardly the idea that the human
> mind is incapable of further advances. This is precisely the doctrine
> which the present despots of the earth are inculcating, and their friends
> here re-echoing; and applying especially to religion and politics; "that it
> is not probable that anything better will be discovered than what was
> known to our fathers." . . . But thank heaven the American mind is
> already too much opened to listen to these impostures, and while the
> art of printing is left to us, science can never be retrograde. . . . To
> preserve the freedom of the human mind . . . every spirit should be
> ready to devote itself to martyrdom. . . . But that the enthusiasm which
> characterizes youth should lift its parricide hands against freedom and
> science would be such a monstrous phenomenon as I could not place
> among the possible things in this age and country.

That is the hard kernel, the seed from which the American dream
would grow into unpruned luxuriance. Jefferson's voice is not remote
from many European voices of his time, but it stands in unique relation to the country to whom he spoke. That attitude was bred into
the bone of America, and in various, often distorted, ways, it has
lasted. Perhaps that is where the trouble begins, for if these virtues of
the American imagination have the elements of greatness in them, they
call immediately for discriminating and practical correctives. The
reality in such an attitude lies in its faith in life; the illusion lies in
the undiscriminating multiplication of its material possibilities.

The Great Gatsby is an exploration of the American dream as it
exists in a corrupt period, and it is an attempt to determine that concealed boundary that divides the reality from the illusions. The illusions seem more real than the reality itself. Embodied in the subordi-
nate characters in the novel, they threaten to invade the whole of the
picture. On the other hand, the reality is embodied in Gatsby; and as
opposed to the hard, tangible illusions, the reality is a thing of the
spirit, a promise rather than the possession of a vision, a faith in the
half-glimpsed, but hardly understood, possibilities of life. In Gatsby's
America, the reality is undefined to itself. It is inarticulate and frustrated. Nick Carraway, Gatsby's friend and Fitzgerald's narrator, says
of Gatsby:

> Through all he said, even through his appalling sentimentality, I was
> reminded of something—an elusive rhythm, a fragment of lost words,

that I had heard somewhere a long time ago. For a moment a phrase tried to take shape in my mouth and my lips parted like a dumb man's, as though there was more struggling upon them than a wisp of startled air. But they made no sound, and what I had almost remembered was incommunicado forever.

This is not pretentious phrase-making performing a vague gesture towards some artificial significance. It is both an evocative and an exact description of that unholy cruel paradox by which the conditions of American history have condemned the grandeur of the aspiration and vision to expend itself in a waste of shame and silence. But the reality is not entirely lost. It ends by redeeming the human spirit, even though it live in a wilderness of illusions, from the cheapness and vulgarity that encompass it. In this novel, the illusions are known and condemned at last simply by the rank complacency with which they are content to be themselves. On the other hand, the reality is in the energy of the spirit's resistance, which may not recognize itself as resistance at all, but which can neither stoop to the illusions nor abide with them when they are at last recognized. Perhaps it is really nothing more than ultimate immunity from the final contamination, but it encompasses the difference between life and death. Gatsby never succeeds in seeing through the sham of his world or his acquaintances very clearly. It is of the essence of his romantic American vision that it should lack the seasoned powers of discrimination. But it invests those illusions with its own faith, and thus it discovers its projected goodness in the frauds of its crippled world. *The Great Gatsby* becomes the acting out of the tragedy of the American vision. It is a vision totally untouched by the scales of values that order life in a society governed by traditional manners; and Fitzgerald knows that although it would be easy to condemn and "place" the illusions by invoking these outside values, to do so would be to kill the reality that lies beyond them, but which can sometimes only be reached through them.

For example, Fitzgerald perfectly understood the inadequacy of Gatsby's romantic view of wealth. But that is not the point. He presents it in Gatsby as a romantic baptism of desire for a reality that stubbornly remains out of his sight. It is as if a savage islander, suddenly touched with Grace, transcended in his prayers and aspirations the grotesque little fetish in which he imagined he discovered the object of his longing. The scene in which Gatsby shows his piles of beautiful imported shirts to Daisy and Nick has been mentioned as a failure of Gatsby's, and so of Fitzgerald's, critical control of values. Actually, the shirts are sacramentals, and it is clear that Gatsby shows them, neither in vanity nor in pride, but with a reverential humility in the presence of some inner vision he cannot consciously grasp, but toward which he desperately struggles in the only way he knows.

In an essay called "Myths for Materialists" Mr. Jacques Barzun once wrote that figures, whether of fact or fiction, insofar as they express destinies, aspirations, attitudes typical of man or particular groups, are invested with a mythical character. In this sense Gatsby is a "mythic" character, and no other word will define him. Not only is he an embodiment (as Fitzgerald makes clear at the outset) of that conflict between illusion and reality at the heart of American life; he is an heroic personification of the American romantic hero, the true heir of the American dream. "There was something gorgeous about him," Nick Carraway says, and although "gorgeous" was a favorite word with the 'twenties, Gatsby wears it with an archetypal American elegance.

One need not look far in earlier American literature to find his forebears. Here is the description of a young bee hunter from *Col. David Crockett's Exploits and Adventures in Texas,* published in 1836:

> I thought myself alone in the street, where the hush of morning was suddenly broken by a clear, joyful, and musical voice, which sang. . . .
>
> I turned toward the spot whence the sounds proceeded, and discovered a tall figure leaning against the sign post. His eyes were fixed on the streaks of light in the east, his mind was absorbed, and he was clearly unconscious of anyone being near him. He continued his song in so full and clear a tone, that the street re-echoed. . . .
>
> I now drew nigh enough to see him distinctly. He was a young man, not more than twenty-two. His figure was light and graceful at the same time that it indicated strength and activity. He was dressed in a hunting shirt, which was made with uncommon neatness, and ornamented tastily with fringe. He held a highly finished rifle in his right hand, and a hunting pouch, covered with Indian ornaments, was slung across his shoulders. His clean shirt collar was open, secured only by a black riband around his neck. His boots were polished, without a soil upon them; and on his head was a neat fur cap, tossed on in a manner which said, "I don't give a d--n," just as plainly as any cap could speak it. I thought it must be some popinjay on a lark, until I took a look at his countenance. It was handsome, bright, and manly. There was no mistake in that face. From the eyes down to the breast he was sunburnt as dark as mahogany while the upper part of his high forehead was as white and polished as marble. Thick clusters of black hair curled from under his cap. I passed on unperceived, and he continued his song. . . .

This young dandy of the frontier, dreaming in the dawn and singing to the morning, is a progenitor of Gatsby. It is because of such a traditional American ancestry that Gatsby's romanticism transcends the limiting glamor of the Jazz Age.

But such a romanticism is not enough to "mythicize" Gatsby. Gatsby, for all his shimmer of representative surfaces, is never allowed to become soiled by the touch of realism. In creating him, Fitzgerald observed as high a decorum of character as a Renaissance playwright: for Gatsby's parents were shiftless and unsuccessful farm people, Gatsby really "sprang from his Platonic conception of himself. He was a son of God—a phrase which, if it means anything, means just that—and he must be about His Father's business, the service of a vast, vulgar, meretricious beauty."

Fitzgerald created Gatsby with a sense of his own election; but the beauty it was in his nature to serve had already been betrayed by history. Even in the midst of the blighted earthly paradise of West Egg, Long Island, Gatsby bore about him the marks of his birth. He is a kind of exiled Duke in disguise. We know him by his bearing, the decorous pattern of his speech. Even his dress invariably touches the imagination: "Gatsby in a white flannel suit, silver shirt, and gold colored tie. . . ." There is something dogmatically Olympic about the combination. After Gatsby's death when his pathetic old father journeys east for the funeral, one feels that he is only the kindly shepherd who once found a baby on the cold hillside.

But so far I have been talking in general terms. This beautiful control of conventions can be studied more closely in the description of Gatsby's party at which (if we except that distant glimpse of him at the end of Chapter I, of which I shall speak later) we encounter him for the first time. We are told later that Gatsby was gifted with a "hint of the unreality of reality, a promise that the rock of the world was founded securely on a fairy's wing." Fitzgerald does not actually let us meet Gatsby face to face until he has concretely created this fantastic world of Gatsby's vision, for it is the element in which we must meet Gatsby if we are to understand his impersonal significance:

> There was music from my neighbor's house through the summer nights. In his blue gardens men and girls came and went like moths among the whisperings and the champagne and the stars. At high tide in the afternoon I watched his guests diving from the tower of his raft, or taking the sun on the hot sand of his beach while his two motor-boats slit the waters of the Sound, drawing aquaplanes over cataracts of foam. On week-ends his Rolls-Royce became an omnibus, bearing parties to and from the city between nine in the morning and long past midnight, while his station wagon scampered like a brisk yellow bug to meet all trains. And on Mondays eight servants, including an extra gardener, toiled all day with mops and scrubbing-brushes and hammers and garden-shears, repairing the ravages of the night before.

The nostalgic poetic quality, which tends to leave one longing for sterner stuff, is, in fact, deceptive. It is Gatsby's ordeal that he must separate the foul dust that floated in the wake of his dreams from the reality of the dream itself: that he must find some vantage point from which he can bring the responsibilities and the possibilities of life into a single focus. But the "ineffable gaudiness" of the world to which Gatsby is committed is a fatal deterrent. Even within the compass of this paragraph we see how the focus has become blurred: how the possibilities of life are conceived of in material terms. But in that heroic list of the vaster luxury items—motor-boats, aquaplanes, private beaches, Rolls-Royces, diving towers—Gatsby's vision maintains its gigantic unreal stature. It imposes a rhythm on his guests which they accept in terms of their own tawdry illusions, having no conception of the compulsion that drives him to offer them the hospitality of his fabulous wealth. They come for their weekends as George Dane in Henry James's *The Great Good Place* went into his dream retreat. But the result is not the same: "on Mondays eight servants, including an extra gardener, toiled all day with mops and scrubbing-brushes and hammers and garden-shears, repairing the ravages of the night before." That is the most important sentence in the paragraph, and despite the fairy-story overtone, it possesses an ironic nuance that rises toward the tragic. And how fine that touch of the extra gardener is— as if Gatsby's guests had made a breach in nature. It completely qualifies the over-fragility of the moths and champagne and blue gardens in the opening sentences.

This theme of the relation of his guests to Gatsby is still further pursued in Chapter IV. The cataloguing of American proper names with poetic intention has been an ineffectual cliché in American writing for many generations. But Fitzgerald uses the convention magnificently:

> Once I wrote down on the empty spaces of a time-table the names of those who came to Gatsby's house that summer. It is an old time-table now, disintegrating at its folds, and headed "This schedule in effect July 5th, 1922." But I can still read the gray names, and they will give you a better impression than my generalities of those who accepted Gatsby's hospitality and paid him the subtle tribute of knowing nothing about him.

The names of these guests could have been recorded nowhere else as appropriately as in the margins of a faded timetable. The embodiments of illusions, they are as ephemeral as time itself; but because their illusions represent the distortions and shards of some shattered American dream, the timetable they adorn is "in effect July 5th"—the day following the great national festival when the exhausted holiday crowds, as spent as exploded firecrackers, return to their homes. The list of names which Fitzgerald proceeds to enumerate conjures up with remarkable precision an atmosphere of vulgar American fortunes and vulgar American destinies. Those who are familiar with the social registers, business men's directories, and movie magazines of the 'twenties might be able to analyze the exact way in which Fitzgerald achieves his effect, but it is enough to say here that he shares with Eliot a remarkable clairvoyance in seizing the cultural implications of proper names. After two pages and more, the list ends with the dreamily elegiac close: "All these people came to Gatsby's house in the summer."

Why did they come? There is the answer of the plotted story—the free party, the motor-boats, the private beach, the endless flow of cocktails. But in the completed pattern of the novel one knows that they came for another reason—came blindly and instinctively—illusions in pursuit of a reality from which they have become historically separated, but by which they might alone be completed or fulfilled. And why did Gatsby invite them? As contrasted with them, he alone has a sense of the reality that hovers somewhere out of sight in this nearly ruined American dream; but the reality is unintelligible until he can invest it again with the tangible forms of his world, and relate it to the logic of history. Gatsby and his guests feel a mutual need of each other, but the division in American experience has widened too far, and no party, no hospitality however lavish, can heal the breach. The illusions and the reality go their separate ways. Gatsby stands at the door of his mansion, in one of the most deeply moving and significant paragraphs of the novel, to wish his guests good-bye:

> The caterwauling horns had reached a crescendo and I turned away and cut across the lawn toward home. I glanced back once. A wafer of a moon was shining over Gatsby's house, making the night fine as before, and surviving the laughter and the sound of his still glowing garden. A sudden emptiness seemed to flow now from the windows and the great doors, endowing with complete isolation the figure of the host, who stood on the porch, his hand up in a formal gesture of farewell.

If one turns back to Davy Crockett's description of the elegant young bee hunter, singing while the dawn breaks in the east, and thinks of it in relation with this midnight picture of Gatsby, "his hand up in a formal gesture of farewell," while the last guests depart through the debris of the finished party, the quality of the romanticism seems much the same, but the situation is exactly reversed; and from the latter scene there opens a perspective of profound meaning. Suddenly Gatsby is not merely a likable, romantic hero; he is a creature of myth in whom is incarnated the aspiration and the ordeal of his race.

"Mythic" characters are impersonal. There is no distinction between their public and their private lives. Because they share their meaning with everyone, they have no secrets and no hidden corners into which they can retire for a moment, unobserved. An intimacy so universal stands revealed in a ritual pattern for the inspection and instruction of the race. The "mythic" character can never withdraw from that air which is his existence—that is to say, from that area of consciousness (and hence of publicity) which every individual shares with the members, both living and dead, of his group or race. Gatsby is a "mythic" character in this sense—he has no private life, no meaning or significance that depends on the fulfillment of his merely private destiny, his happiness as an individual in a society of individuals. In a transcendent sense he touches our imaginations, but in this smaller sense—which is the world of the realistic novel—he even fails to arouse our curiosity. At this level, his love affair with Daisy is too easily "placed," a tawdry epic "crush" of no depth or interest in itself. But Gatsby not only remains undiminished by what is essentially the meanness of the affair: his stature grows, as we watch, to the proportions of a hero. We must inquire how Fitzgerald managed this extraordinary achievement.

Daisy Buchanan exists at two well-defined levels in the novel. She is what she is—but she exists also at the level of Gatsby's vision of her. The intelligence of no other important novelist has been as consistently undervalued as Fitzgerald's, and it is hardly surprising that no critic has ever given Fitzgerald credit for his superb understanding of Daisy's vicious emptiness. Even Fitzgerald's admirers regard Daisy as rather a good, if somewhat silly, little thing; but Fitzgerald knew that at its most depraved levels the American dream merges with the American debutante's dream—a thing of deathly hollowness. Fitzgerald faces up squarely to the problem of telling us what Daisy has to offer in a human relationship. At one of Gatsby's fabulous parties— the one to which Daisy brings her husband, Tom Buchanan—Gatsby points out to Daisy and Tom, among the celebrated guests, one particular couple:

> "Perhaps you know that lady," Gatsby indicated a gorgeous, scarcely human orchid of a woman who sat in state under a white-plum tree. Tom and Daisy stared, with that peculiarly unreal feeling that accompanies the recognition of a hitherto ghostly celebrity of the movies.
> "She's lovely," said Daisy.
> "The man bending over her is her director."

Superficially, the scene is highly civilized. One fancies one has seen it in Manet. But in the context we know that it has no reality whatever—the star and her director can get no nearer reality than by rehearsing a scene. Out attention is then taken up by other scenes at the party, but by suddenly returning to this couple after an interval of two pages to make his point, Fitzgerald achieves a curious impression of static or arrested action. We have the feeling that if we walked behind the white-plum tree we should only see the back of a canvas screen:

> Almost the last thing I remember was standing with Daisy and watching the moving-picture director and his Star. They were still under the white-plum tree and their faces were touching except for a pale, thin ray of moonlight between. It occurred to me that he had been very slowly bending toward her all evening to attain this proximity, and even while I watched I saw him stoop one ultimate degree and kiss at her cheek.
> "I like her," said Daisy, "I think she's lovely."
> But the rest offended her—and inarguably, because it wasn't a gesture but an emotion.

Daisy likes the moving-picture actress because she has no substance. She is a gesture that is committed to nothing more real than her own image on the silver screen. She has become a gesture divorced forever from the tiresomeness of human rality. In effect, this passage is Daisy's confession of faith. She virtually announces here what her criteria of human emotions and conduct are. Fitzgerald's illustration of the emptiness of Daisy's character—an emptiness that we see curdling into the viciousness of a monstrous moral indifference as the story unfolds —is drawn with a fineness and depth of critical understanding, and communicated with a force of imagery so rare in modern American writing, that it is almost astonishing that he is often credited with giving in to those very qualities which *The Great Gatsby* so effectively excoriates.

But what is the basis for the mutual attraction between Daisy and Gatsby? In Daisy's case the answer is simple. We remember that Nick Carraway has described Gatsby's personality as an "unbroken series of successful gestures." Superficially, Daisy finds in Gatsby, or thinks she finds, that safety from human reality which the empty gesture implies. What she fails to realize is that Gatsby's gorgeous gesturings are the reflex of an aspiration toward the possibilities of life, and this is something entirely different from those vacant images of romance and sophistication that fade so easily into the nothingness from which they came. But in a sense, Daisy is safe enough from the reality she dreads. The true question is not what Gatsby sees in Daisy, but the direction he takes from her, what he sees *beyond* her; and that has, despite the immaturity intrinsic in Gatsby's vision, an element of grandeur in it. For Gatsby, Daisy does not exist in herself. She is the green light that signals him into the heart of his ultimate vision. *Why* she should have this evocative power over Gatsby is a question Fitzgerald faces beautifully and successfully as he recreates that milieu of uncritical snobbishness and frustrated idealism—monstrous fusion—which is the world in which Gatsby is compelled to live.

Fitzgerald, then, has a sure control when he defines the quality of this love affair. He shows it in itself as vulgar and specious. It has no possible interest in its own right, and if it did have the pattern of the novel would be ruined. Our imaginations would be fettered in those details and interests which would detain us on the narrative level where the affair works itself out as human history, and Gatsby would lose his "mythic" quality. But the economy with which Gatsby is presented, the formal and boldly drawn structural lines of his imagination, lead us at once to a level where it is obvious that Daisy's significance in the story lies in her failure to represent the objective correlative of Gatsby's vision. And at the same time, Daisy's wonderfully representative quality as a creature of the Jazz Age relates her personal failure to the larger failure of Gatsby's society to satisfy his need. In fact, Fitzgerald never allows Daisy's failure to become a human or personal one. He maintains it with sureness on a symbolic level where it is identified with and reflects the failure of Gatsby's decadent American world. There is a famous passage in which Gatsby sees Daisy as an embodiment of the glamor of wealth. Nick Carraway is speaking first to Gatsby:

> "She's got an indiscreet voice," I remarked. "It's full of—" I hesitated.
> "Her voice is full of money," he said suddenly.
> That was it. I'd never understood before. It was full of money—that was the inexhaustible charm that rose and fell in it, the jingle of it, the cymbals' song of it. . . . High in a white palace the king's daughter, the golden girl . . .

Gatsby tries to build up the inadequacy of each value by the support of the other; but united they fall as wretchedly short of what he is seeking as each does singly. Gatsby's gold and Gatsby's girl belong to the fairy story in which the Princess spins whole rooms of money from skeins of wool. In the fairy story, the value never lies in the gold but in something beyond. And so it is in this story. For Gatsby, Daisy is only the promise of fulfillment that lies beyond the green light that burns all night on her dock.

This green light that is visible at night across the bay from the windows and lawn of Gatsby's house is the central symbol in the book. Significantly, our first glimpse of Gatsby at the end of Chapter I is related to it. Nick Carraway, whose modest bungalow in West Egg stands next to Gatsby's mansion, returning from an evening at the Buchanans', while lingering on the lawn for a final moment under the stars, becomes aware that he is not alone:

> . . . fifty feet away a figure had emerged from the shadow of my neighbor's mansion and was standing with his hands in his pockets regarding the silver pepper of the stars. Something in his leisurely movements and the secure position of his feet upon the lawn suggested that it was Mr. Gatsby himself, come out to determine what share was his of our local heavens.
>
> I decided to call to him. . . . But I didn't . . . for he gave a sudden intimation that he was content to be alone—he stretched out his arms toward the dark water in a curious way, and, as far as I was from him, I could have sworn he was trembling. Involuntarily I glanced seaward—and distinguished nothing except a single green light, minute and far away, that might have been the end of a dock. When I looked once more for Gatsby he had vanished, and I was alone again in the unquiet darkness.

It is hardly too much to say that the whole being of Gatsby exists only in relation to what the green light symbolizes. This first sight we have of Gatsby is a ritualistic tableau that literally contains the meaning of the completed book, although the full meaning of what is implicit in the symbol reveals itself slowly, and is only finally rounded out on the last page. We have a fuller definition of what the green light means in its particular, as opposed to its universal, signification in Chapter V. Gatsby is speaking to Daisy as they stand at one of the windows of his mansion:

> "If it wasn't for the mist we could see your home across the bay," said Gatsby. "You always have a green light that burns all night at the end of your dock."
>
> Daisy put her arm through his abruptly, but he seemed absorbed in what he had just said. Possibly it had occurred to him that the colossal significance of that light had now vanished forever. Compared to the great distance that had separated him from Daisy it had seemed very near to her, almost touching her. It had seemed as close as a star to the moon. Now it was again a green light on a dock. His count of enchanted objects had diminished by one.

Some might object to this symbolism on the grounds that it is easily vulgarized—as A. J. Cronin has proved. But if studied carefully in its full context it represents a convincing achievement. The tone or pitch of the symbol is exactly adequate to the problem it dramatizes. Its immediate function is that it signals Gatsby into his future, away from the cheapness of his affair with Daisy which he has vainly tried (and desperately continues trying) to create in the image of his vision. The green light is successful because, apart from its visual effectiveness as it gleams across the bay, it embodies the profound naiveté of Gatsby's sense of the future, while simultaneously suggesting the historicity of his hope. This note of historicity is not fully apparent at this point, of course. The symbol occurs several times, and most notably at the end:

> Gatsby believed in the green light, the orgastic future that year by year recedes before us. It eluded us then, but that's no matter—tomorrow we will run faster, stretch out our arms farther. . . . And one fine morning—
> So we beat on, boats against the current, borne back ceaselessly into the past.

Thus the American dream, whose superstitious valuation of the future began in the past, gives the green light through which alone the American returns to his traditional roots, paradoxically retreating into the pattern of history while endeavoring to exploit the possibilities of the future. There is a suggestive echo of the past in Gatsby's sense of Daisy. He had known her, and fallen in love with her, five years before the novel opens. During that long interval while they had disappeared from each other's sight, Daisy has become a legend in Gatsby's memory, a part of his private past which (as a "mythic" character) he assimilates into the pattern of that historic past through which he would move into the historic future. But the legendary Daisy, meeting her after five years, has dimmed a little in luster:

> "And she doesn't understand," he said. "She used to be able to understand. We'd sit for hours—"
> He broke off and began to walk up and down a desolate path of fruit rinds and discarded favors and crushed flowers.
> "I wouldn't ask too much of her," I ventured. "You can't repeat the past."
> "Can't repeat the past?" he cried incredulously. "Why of course you can!"
> He looked around him wildly, as if the past were lurking here in the shadow of his house, just out of reach of his hand.

By such passages Fitzgerald dramatizes Gatsby's symbolic role. The American dream, stretched between a golden past and a golden future, is always betrayed by a desolate present—a moment of fruit rinds and discarded favors and crushed flowers. Imprisoned in his present, Gatsby belongs even more to the past than to the future. His aspirations have been rehearsed, and his tragedy suffered, by all the generations of Americans who have gone before. His sense of the future, of the possibilities of life, he has learned from the dead.

If we return to the passage in which, linked arm in arm, Gatsby and Daisy stand at the window looking toward the green light across the bay, it may be possible to follow a little more sympathetically that quality of disillusion which begins to creep into Gatsby's response to life. It does not happen because of the impoverished elements of his practical romance: it happens because Gatsby is incapable of compromising with his inner vision. The imagery of this particular passage, as I suggested, is gauged to meet the requirements of Gatsby's young romantic dream. But two pages later Fitzgerald takes up the theme of Gatsby's struggle against disenchantment once again, and this time in an imagery that suggests how much he had learned from *The Waste Land*:

> When Klipspringer had played "The Love Nest" he turned around on the bench and searched unhappily for Gatsby in the gloom.
>
> "I'm all out of practice, you see. I told you I couldn't play. I'm all out of prac—"
>
> "Don't talk so much, old sport," commanded Gatsby. "Play!"
>
> > *In the morning,*
> > *In the evening,*
> > *Ain't we got fun—*
>
> Outside the wind was loud and there was a faint flow of thunder along the Sound. All the lights were going on in West Egg now; the electric trains, men-carrying, were plunging home through the rain from New York. It was the hour of a profound human change, and excitement was generating on the air.
>
> > *One thing's sure and nothing's surer*
> > *The rich get richer and the poor get—children.*
> > *In the meantime,*
> > *In between time—*
>
> As I went over to say good-by I saw that the expression of bewilderment had come back into Gatsby's face, as though a faint doubt had occurred to him as to the quality of his present happiness. Almost five years! There must have been moments even that afternoon when Daisy tumbled short of his dreams—not through her own fault, but because of the colossal vitality of his illusion. It had gone beyond her, beyond everything. He had thrown himself into it with a creative passion, adding to it all the time, decking it out with every bright feather that drifted his

way. No amount of fire or freshness can challenge what a man can store up in his ghostly heart.

In view of such writing it is absurd to argue that Fitzgerald's art was a victim of his own attraction to the Jazz Age. The snatches of song that Klipspringer sings evoke the period with an immediacy that is necessary if we are to understand the peculiar poignancy of Gatsby's ordeal. But the songs are more than evocative. They provide the ironic musical prothalamion for Gatsby's romance, and as Gatsby listens to them an intimation of the practical truth presses in on him. The recognition is heightened poetically by that sense of the elements, the faint flow of thunder along the Sound, which forms the background of those artificial little tunes. And it is not odd that this evocation of the outdoor scene, while Klipspringer pounds at the piano inside, sustains in the imagination the image of that green light, symbol of Gatsby's faith, which is burning across the bay. This scene draws on the "violet hour" passage from "The Fire Sermon" in which "the human engine waits/Like a taxi throbbing waiting. . . ." It is the hour of a profound human change, and in the faint stirrings of Gatsby's recognition there is for a moment, perhaps, a possibility of his escape. But the essence of the American dream whose tragedy Gatsby is enacting is that it lives in a past and a future that never existed, and is helpless in the present that does.

Gatsby's opposite number in the story is Daisy's husband, Tom Buchanan, and Gatsby's stature—his touch of doomed but imperishable spiritual beauty, if I may call it so—is defined by his contrast with Tom. In many ways they are analogous in their characteristics—just sufficiently so to point up the differences. For example, their youth is an essential quality of them both. But Tom Buchanan was "one of those men who reach such an acute limited excellence at twenty-one that everything afterward savors of anti-climax." Even his body— "a body capable of enormous leverage"—was "a cruel body." In the description of Tom we are left physically face to face with a scion of those ruthless generations who raised up the great American fortunes, and who now live in uneasy arrogant leisure on their brutal acquisitions. But Gatsby's youth leaves an impression of interminability. Its climax is always in the future, and it gives rather than demands. Its energy is not in its body, but in its spirit, and meeting Gatsby for the first time, one seizes, as Nick Carraway did, this impression in his smile:

> It was one of those rare smiles with a quality of eternal reassurance in it, that you may come across four or five times in life. It faced—or seemed to face—the whole external world for an instant, and then concentrated on *you* with an irresistible prejudice in your favor. It under-

stood you just as far as you wanted to be understood, believed in you
as you would like to believe in yourself, and assured you that it had precisely the impression of you that, at your best, you hoped to convey.
Precisely at that point it vanished—and I was looking at an elegant
young rough-neck, a year or two over thirty, whose elaborate formality
of speech just missed being absurd.

This passage is masterly in the way in which it presents Gatsby to
us less as an individual than as a projection, or mirror, of our ideal
selves. To do that is the function of all "mythic" characters. Gatsby's
youth is not simply a matter of three decades that will quickly multiply
themselves into four or five. It is a quality of faith and hope that may
be betrayed by history, may be killed by society, but that no exposure
to the cynical turns of time can reduce to the compromises of age.

Again, Gatsby and Tom are alike in the possession of a certain
sentimentality, but Tom Buchanan's is based on depraved self-pity.
He is never more typical than when coaxing himself to tears over a
half-finished box of dog biscuits that recalls a drunken and illicit day
from his past, associated in memory with his dead mistress. His self-
pity is functional. It is sufficient to condone his most criminal acts in
his own eyes as long as the crimes are not imputable. But Gatsby's
sentimentality exists in the difficulty of expressing, in the phrases and
symbols provided by his decadent society, the reality that lies at the
heart of his aspiration. "So he waited, listening for a moment longer
to the tuning fork that had been struck upon a star"—Gatsby's sentimentality (if it *is* sentimentality, and I rather doubt it) is as innocent
as that. It has nothing of self-pity or indulgence in it—it is all aspiration and goodness; and it must be remembered that Fitzgerald himself
is *outside* Gatsby's vocabulary, using it with great mastery to convey
the poignancy of the situation.

Tom Buchanan and Gatsby represent antagonistic but historically
related aspects of America. They are related as the body and the soul
when a mortal barrier has risen up between them. Tom Buchanan is
virtually Gatsby's murderer in the end, but the crime that he commits
by proxy is only a symbol of his deeper spiritual crime against Gatsby's
inner vision. Gatsby's guilt, insofar as it exists, is radical failure—a
failure of the critical faculty that seems to be an inherent part of the
American dream—to understand that Daisy is as fully immersed in
the destructive element of the American world as Tom himself. After
Daisy, while driving Gatsby's white automobile, has killed Mrs. Wilson
and, implicitly at least, left Gatsby to shoulder the blame, Nick
Carraway gives us a crucial insight into the spiritual affinity of the
Buchanan couple, drawing together in their callous selfishness in a
moment of guilt and crisis:

Daisy and Tom were sitting opposite each other at the kitchen table with a plate of cold fried chicken between them, and two bottles of ale. He was talking intently across the table at her, and in his earnestness his hand had fallen upon and covered her own. Once in a while she looked up at him and nodded in agreement.

They weren't happy, and neither of them had touched the chicken or the ale—and yet they weren't unhappy either. There was an unmistakable air of natural intimacy about the picture, and anybody would have said that they were conspiring together.

They instinctively seek out each other because each recognizes the other's strength in the corrupt spiritual element they inhabit.

There is little point in tracing out in detail the implications of the action any further, although it could be done with an exactness approaching allegory. That it is not allegory is owing to the fact that the pattern emerges from the fullness of Fitzgerald's living experience of his own society and time. In the end the most that can be said is that *The Great Gatsby* is a dramatic affirmation in fictional terms of the American spirit in the midst of an American world that denies the soul. Gatsby exists in, and for, that affirmation alone. When, at the end, not even Gatsby can hide his recognition of the speciousness of his dream any longer, the discovery is made in universalizing terms that dissolve Daisy into the larger world she has stood for in Gatsby's imagination:

He must have looked up at an unfamiliar sky through frightening leaves and shivered as he found what a grotesque thing a rose is and how raw the sunlight was upon the scarcely created grass. A new world, material without being real, where poor ghosts, breathing dreams like air, drifted fortuitously about. . . .

"A new world, material without being real." Paradoxically, it was Gatsby's dream that conferred reality upon the world. The reality was in his faith in the goodness of creation, and in the possibilities of life. That these possibilities were intrinsically related to such romantic components limited and distorted his dream, and finally left it helpless in the face of the Buchanans, but it did not corrupt it. When the dream melted, it knocked the prop of reality from under the universe, and face to face with the physical substance at last, Gatsby realized that the illusion was *there*—there where Tom and Daisy, and generations of small-minded, ruthless Americans had found it—in the dreamless, visionless complacency of mere matter, substance without form. After this recognition, Gatsby's death is only a symbolic formality, for the world into which his mere body had been born rejected the gift he had been created to embody—the traditional dream from which alone it could awaken into life.

As the novel closes, the experience of Gatsby and his broken dream explicitly becomes the focus of that historic dream for which he stands. Nick Carraway is speaking:

> Most of the big shore places were closed now and there were hardly any lights except the shadowy, moving glow of a ferryboat across the Sound. And as the moon rose higher the inessential houses began to melt away until gradually I became aware of the old island here that flowered once for Dutch sailors' eyes—a fresh, green breast of the new world. Its vanished trees, the trees that had once made way for Gatsby's house, had once pandered in whispers to the last and greatest of all human dreams; for a transitory enchanted moment man must have held his breath in the presence of this continent, compelled into an aesthetic contemplation he neither understood nor desired, face to face for the last time in history with something commensurate to his capacity for wonder.

It is fitting that this, like so many of the others in *Gatsby*, should be a moonlight scene, for the history and the romance are one. Gatsby fades into the past forever to take his place with the Dutch sailors who had chosen their moment in time so much more happily than he. We recognize that the great achievement of this novel is that it manages, while poetically evoking a sense of the goodness of that early dream, to offer the most damaging criticism of it in American literature. The astonishing thing is that the criticism—if indictment wouldn't be the better word—manages to be part of the tribute. Gatsby, the "mythic" embodiment of the American dream, is shown to us in all his immature romanticism. His insecure grasp of social and human values, his lack of critical intelligence and self-knowledge, his blindness to the pitfalls that surround him in American society, his compulsive optimism, are realized in the text with rare assurance and understanding. And yet the very grounding of these deficiencies is Gatsby's goodness and faith in life, his compelling desire to realize all the possibilities of existence, his belief that we can have an Earthly Paradise populated by Buchanans. A great part of Fitzgerald's achievement is that he suggests effectively that these terrifying deficiencies are not so much the private deficiencies of Gatsby, but are deficiencies inherent in contemporary manifestations of the American vision itself—a vision no doubt admirable, but stupidly defenseless before the equally American world of Tom and Daisy. Gatsby's deficiencies of intelligence and judgment bring him to his tragic death—a death that is spiritual as well as physical. But the more important question that faces us through our sense of the immediate tragedy is where they have brought America.

Scott Fitzgerald's Fable of
East and West

by Robert Ornstein

He felt then that if the pilgrimage eastward of the rare poisonous flower of his race was the end of the adventure which had started westward three hundred years ago, if the long serpent of the curiosity had turned too sharp upon itself, cramping its bowels, bursting its shining skin, at least there had been a journey; like to the satisfaction of a man coming to die—one of those human things that one can never understand unless one has made such a journey and heard the man give thanks with the husbanded breath. The frontiers were gone—there were no more barbarians. The short gallop of the last great race, the polyglot, the hated and the despised, the crass and scorned, had gone—at least it was not a meaningless extinction up an alley. (*The Crack-Up*, p. 199)

After a brief revival, the novels of Scott Fitzgerald seem destined again for obscurity, labeled this time, by their most recent critics, as darkly pessimistic studies of America's spiritual and ideological failures. *The Great Gatsby*, we are now told, is not simply a chronicle of the Jazz Age but rather a dramatization of the betrayal of the naive American dream in a corrupt society.* I would agree that in *Gatsby* Fitzgerald did create a myth with the imaginative sweep of America's historical adventure across an untamed continent. But his fable of East and West is little concerned with twentieth century materialism and moral anarchy, for its theme is the unending quest of the romantic dream, which is forever betrayed in fact and yet redeemed in men's minds.

From the start, Fitzgerald's personal dreams of romance contained

---

"*Scott Fitzgerald's Fable of East and West*" by Robert Ornstein. From College English, *XVIII (1956-57), 139-43. Copyright © 1957 by the National Council of Teachers of English. Reprinted by permission of the NCTE and Robert Ornstein.*

* See Edwin Fussell, "Fitzgerald's Brave New World," *ELH*, XIX (Dec. 1952), 291-306; Marius Bewley, "Scott Fitzgerald's Criticism of America," *SR*, LXII (Spring 1954), 223-246; John W. Bicknell, "The Wasteland of F. Scott Fitzgerald," *VQR*, XXX (Autumn 1954). A somewhat different but equally negative interpretation is R. W. Stallman's "Gatsby and the Hole in Time," *MFS*, I (Nov. 1955), 1-15.

the seeds of their own destruction. In his earliest works, his optimistic sense of the value of experience is overshadowed by a personal intuition of tragedy; his capacity for naive wonder is chastened by satiric and ironic insights which make surrender to the romantic impulse incomplete. Though able to idealize the sensuous excitement of an exclusive party or a lovely face, Fitzgerald could not ignore the speciosity inherent in the romantic stimuli of his social world—in the unhurried gracious poise that money can buy. Invariably he studied what fascinated him so acutely that he could give at times a clinical report on the very rich, whose world seemed to hold the promise of a life devoid of the vulgar and commonplace. A literalist of his own imagination (and therefore incapable of self-deception), he peopled extravagant phantasy with superbly real "denizens of Broadway." The result in the earlier novels is not so much an uncertainty of tone as a curious alternation of satiric and romantic moments—a breathless adoration of flapper heroines whose passionate kisses are tinged with frigidity and whose daring freedom masks an adolescent desire for the reputation rather than the reality of experience.

The haunting tone of *Gatsby* is more than a skilful fusion of Fitzgerald's satiric and romantic contrarieties. Nick Carraway, simultaneously enchanted and repelled by the variety of life, attains Fitzgerald's mature realization that the protective enchantment of the romantic ideal lies in its remoteness from actuality. He knows the fascination of yellow windows high above the city streets even as he looks down from Myrtle Wilson's gaudy, smoke-filled apartment. He still remembers the initial wonder of Gatsby's parties long after he is sickened by familiarity with Gatsby's uninvited guests. In one summer Nick discovers a profoundly melancholy esthetic truth: that romance belongs not to the present but to a past transfigured by imagined memory and to the illusory promise of an unrealizable future. Gatsby, less wise than Nick, destroys himself in an attempt to seize the green light in his own fingers.

At the same time that Fitzgerald perceived the melancholy nature of romantic illusion, his attitude towards the very rich crystalized. In *Gatsby* we see that the charming irresponsibility of the flapper has developed into the criminal amorality of Daisy Buchanan, and that the smug conceit of the Rich Boy has hardened into Tom Buchanan's arrogant cruelty. We know in retrospect that Anthony Patch's tragedy was not his "poverty," but his possession of the weakness and purposelessness of the very rich without their protective armor of wealth.

The thirst for money is a crucial motive in *Gatsby* as in Fitzgerald's other novels, and yet none of his major characters are materialists, for money is never their final goal. The rich are too accustomed to money to covet it. It is simply the badge of their "superiority" and the justifi-

cation of their consuming snobberies. For those who are not very rich
—for the Myrtle Wilsons as well as the Jay Gatsbys—it is the alchemic
reagent that transmutes the ordinary worthlessness of life. Money is
the demiurgos of Jimmy Gatz's Platonic universe, and the proof, in
"Babylon Revisited," of the unreality of reality (". . . the snow of
twenty-nine wasn't real snow. If you didn't want it to be snow, you
just paid some money"). Even before *Gatsby*, in "The Rich Boy,"
Fitzgerald had defined the original sin of the very rich: They do not
worship material gods, but they "possess and enjoy early, and it does
something to them, makes them soft where we are hard, and cynical
where we are trustful. . . ." Surrounded from childhood by the artificial security of wealth, accustomed to owning rather than wanting,
they lack anxiety or illusion, frustration or fulfillment. Their romantic
dreams are rooted in the adolescence from which they never completely
escape—in the excitement of the prom or petting party, the reputation
of being fast on the college gridiron or the college weekend.

Inevitably, then, Fitzgerald saw his romantic dream threaded by a
double irony. Those who possess the necessary means lack the will,
motive, or capacity to pursue a dream. Those with the heightened
sensitivity to the promises of life have it because they are the dis-
inherited, forever barred from the white palace where "the king's
daughter, the golden girl" awaits "safe and proud above the struggles
of the poor." Amory Blaine loses his girl writing advertising copy at
ninety a month. Anthony Patch loses his mind after an abortive
attempt to recoup his fortune peddling bonds. Jay Gatsby loses his
life even though he makes his millions because they are not the kind
of safe, respectable money that echoes in Daisy's lovely voice. The
successful entrepreneurs of Gatsby's age are the panderers to vulgar
tastes, the high pressure salesmen, and, of course, the bootleggers. Yet
once, Fitzgerald suggests, there had been opportunity commensurate
with aspiration, an unexplored and unexploited frontier where great
fortunes had been made or at least romantically stolen. And out of
the shifting of opportunities from the West to Wall Street, he creates
an American fable which redeems as well as explains romantic failure.

But how is one to accept, even in fable, a West characterized by the
dull rectitude of Minnesota villages and an East epitomized by the
sophisticated dissipation of Long Island society? The answer is perhaps
that Fitzgerald's dichotomy of East and West has the poetic truth of
James's antithesis of provincial American virtue and refined European
sensibility. Like *The Portrait of a Lady* and *The Ambassadors, Gatsby*
is a story of "displaced persons" who have journeyed eastward in search
of a larger experience of life. To James this reverse migration from
the New to the Old World has in itself no special significance. To
Fitzgerald, however, the lure of the East represents a profound dis-

placement of the American dream, a turning back upon itself of the historic pilgrimage towards the frontier which had, in fact, created and sustained that dream. In *Gatsby* the once limitless western horizon is circumscribed by the "bored, sprawling, swollen towns beyond the Ohio, with their interminable inquisitions which spared only the children and the very old." The virgin territories of the frontiersman have been appropriated by the immigrant families, the diligent Swedes —the unimaginative, impoverished German farmers like Henry Gatz. Thus after a restless nomadic existence, the Buchanans settle "permanently" on Long Island because Tom would be "a God damned fool to live anywhere else." Thus Nick comes to New York with a dozen volumes on finance which promise "to unfold the shining secrets that only Midas, Morgan and Maecenas knew." Gatsby's green light, of course, shines in only one direction—from the East across the Continent to Minnesota, from the East across the bay to his imitation mansion in West Egg.

Lying in the moonlight on Gatsby's deserted beach, Nick realizes at the close just how lost a pilgrimage Gatsby's had been:

> . . . I became aware of the old island here that had flowered once for Dutch sailors' eyes—a fresh, green breast of the new world. Its vanished trees, the trees that had made way for Gatsby's house, had once pandered in whispers to the last and greatest of all human dreams; for a transitory moment man must have held his breath in the presence of this continent, compelled into an aesthetic contemplation he neither understood nor desired, face to face for the last time in history with something commensurate to his capacity for wonder.

Gatsby is the spiritual descendant of these Dutch sailors. Like them, he set out for gold and stumbled on a dream. But he journeys in the wrong direction in time as well as space. The transitory enchanted moment has come and gone for him and for the others, making the romantic promise of the future an illusory reflection of the past. Nick still carries with him a restlessness born of the war's excitement; Daisy silently mourns the romantic adventure of her "white" girlhood; Tom seeks the thrill of a vanished football game. Gatsby devotes his life to recapturing a love lost five years before. When the present offers nothing commensurate with man's capacity for wonder, the romantic credo is the belief—Gatsby's belief—in the ability to repeat the disembodied past. Each step towards the green light, however, shadows some part of Gatsby's grandiose achievement. With Daisy's disapproval the spectroscopic parties cease. To preserve her reputation Gatsby empties his mansion of lights and servants. And finally only darkness and ghostly memories tenant the deserted house as Gatsby relives his romantic past for Nick after the accident.

Like his romantic dream Jay Gatsby belongs to a vanished past. His career began when he met Dan Cody, a debauched relic of an earlier America who made his millions in the copper strikes. From Cody he received an education in ruthlessness which he applied when the accident of the war brought him to the beautiful house of Daisy Fay. In the tradition of Cody's frontier, he "took what he could get, ravenously and unscrupulously," but in taking Daisy he fell in love with her. "She vanished into her rich house, into her rich full life, leaving Gatsby— nothing. He felt married to her, that was all."

"He felt married to her"—here is the reaction of bourgeois conscience, not of calculating ambition. But then Gatsby is not really Cody's protégé. Jimmy Gatz inherited an attenuated version of the American dream of success, a more moral and genteel dream suited to a nation arriving at the respectability of established wealth and class. Respectability demands that avarice be masked with virtue, that personal aggrandisement pose as self-improvement. Success is no longer to the cutthroat or the ruthless but to the diligent and the industrious, to the boy who scribbles naive resolves on the flyleaf of *Hopalong Cassidy*. Fabricated of pulp fiction clichés (the impoverished materials of an extraordinary imagination), Gatsby's dream of self-improvement blossoms into a preposterous tale of ancestral wealth and culture. And his dream is incorruptible because his great enterprise is not side-street "drugstores," or stolen bonds, but himself, his fictional past, his mansion and his gaudy entertainments. Through it all he moves alone and untouched; he is the impresario, the creator, not the enjoyer of a riotous venture dedicated to an impossible goal.

It may seem ironic that Gatsby's dream of self-improvement is realized through partnership with Meyer Wolfsheim, but Wolfsheim is merely the post-war successor to Dan Cody and to the ruthlessness and greed that once exploited a virgin West. He is the fabulous manipulator of bootleg gin rather than of copper, the modern man of legendary accomplishment "who fixed the World's Series back in 1919." The racketeer, Fitzgerald suggests, is the last great folk hero, the Paul Bunyan of an age in which romantic wonder surrounds underworld "gonnegtions" instead of raw courage or physical strength.   ·
And actually Gatsby is destroyed not by Wolfsheim, or association with him, but by the provincial squeamishness which makes all the Westerners in the novel unadaptable to life in the East.

Despite her facile cynicism and claim to sophistication, Daisy is still the "nice" girl who grew up in Louisville in a beautiful house with a wicker settee on the porch. She remains "spotless," still immaculately dressed in white and capable of a hundred whimsical, vaporous enthusiasms. She has assimilated the urbane ethic of the East which allows a bored wife a casual discreet affair. But she cannot, like

Gatsby's uninvited guests, wink at the illegal and the criminal. When Tom begins to unfold the sordid details of Gatsby's career, she shrinks away; she never intended to leave her husband, but now even an affair is impossible. Tom's provinciality is more boorish than genteel. He has assumed the role of Long Island country gentleman who keeps a mistress in a midtown apartment. But with Myrtle Wilson by his side he turns the role into a ludicrous travesty. By nature a libertine, by upbringing a prig, Tom shatters Gatsby's façade in order to preserve his "gentleman's" conception of womanly virtue and of the sanctity of his marriage.

Ultimately, however, Gatsby is the victim of his own small-town notions of virtue and chivalry. "He would never so much as look at a friend's wife"—or at least he would never try to steal her in her husband's house. He wants Daisy to say that she never loved Tom because only in this way can the sacrament of Gatsby's "marriage" to her in Louisville—his prior claim—be recognized. Not content merely to repeat the past, he must also eradicate the years in which his dream lost its reality. But the dream, like the vanished frontier which it almost comes to represent, is lost forever "somewhere back in that vast obscurity beyond the city, where the dark field of the republic rolled on under the night."

After Gatsby's death Nick prepares to return to his Minnesota home, a place of warmth and enduring stability, carrying with him a surrealistic night vision of the debauchery of the East. Yet his return is not a positive rediscovery of the well-springs of American life. Instead it seems a melancholy retreat from the ruined promise of the East, from the empty present to the childhood memory of the past. Indeed, it is this childhood memory, not the reality of the West which Nick cherishes. For he still thinks the East, despite its nightmarish aspect, superior to the stultifying small-town dullness from which he fled. And by the close of *Gatsby* it is unmistakably clear that the East does not symbolize contemporary decadence and the West the pristine virtues of an earlier America. Fitzgerald does not contrast Gatsby's criminality with his father's unspoiled rustic strength and dignity. He contrasts rather Henry Gatz's dull, grey, almost insentient existence, "a meaningless extinction up an alley," with Gatsby's pilgrimage Eastward, which, though hopeless and corrupting, was at least a journey of life and hope—an escape from the "vast obscurity" of the West that once spawned and then swallowed the American dream. Into this vast obscurity the Buchanans finally disappear. They are not Westerners any longer, or Easterners, but merely two of the very rich, who in the end represent nothing but themselves. They are careless people, Tom and Daisy, selfish, destructive, capable of anything except human sympathy, and yet not sophisticated enough to be really decadent. Their irresponsibility, Nick realizes, is that of pampered children, who smash up "things and creatures . . . and let other people clean up the mess." They live in the eternal moral adolescence which only wealth can produce and protect.

By ignoring its context one can perhaps make much of Nick's indictment of the Buchanans. One can even say that in *The Great Gatsby* Fitzgerald adumbrated the coming tragedy of a nation grown decadent without achieving maturity—a nation that possessed and enjoyed early, and in its arrogant assumption of superiority lost sight of the dream that had created it. But is it not absurd to interpret Gatsby as a mythic Spenglerian anti-hero? Gatsby *is* great, because his dream, however naive, gaudy, and unattainable is one of the grand illusions of the race which keep men from becoming too old or too wise or too cynical of their human limitations. Scott Fitzgerald's fable of East and West does not lament the decline of American civilization. It mourns the eternal lateness of the present hour suspended between the past of romantic memory and the future of romantic promise which ever recedes before us.

The Theme and the Narrator
of *The Great Gatsby*

by *Thomas A. Hanzo*

Of the two most prominent careers which figure in F. Scott Fitzgerald's *The Great Gatsby,* Jay Gatsby's is a variation of the American success story, and Nick Carraway's is an example, differing from others in locale and therefore also in implication, of the provincial American's career in a society more sophisticated than his own.[1] Fitzgerald was able to combine the types through the convention of the first person narration, but Nick's fate has been generally ignored in detailed criticisms of the book. Gatsby and his dream, in these interpretations, are Fitzgerald's subjects, and through them is seen his ultimate subject, "fundamentally, the heterogeneous nature of American culture," as a recent article has it.[2] Lionel Trilling has suggested a use of this conception by Fitzgerald which, by a slight distortion, I should like to develop for my own purposes: "He [Fitzgerald] exaggerated the idea of society and his dependence upon it in order, we may say, to provide a field for the activity of his conscience, for the trial of his self."[3] Gatsby surely represents one of Fitzgerald's trials of self, an incomplete one, however, in contrast with the less dramatic experience of Nick Carraway. Fitzgerald's intention cannot be clarified, nor the significance of his achievement grasped, without our sharing with Nick the trial of his self and the activity of his conscience in that society of which Gatsby is only the most notable part.

"The Theme and the Narrator of The Great Gatsby*" by Thomas A. Hanzo. From* Modern Fiction Studies, *II (Winter, 1956-57), 183-90. Copyright © 1957 by Purdue University-Purdue Research Foundation. Reprinted by permission of* Modern Fiction Studies.

[1] The Americans of Henry James' novels are examples of the type; James dealt, according to Yvor Winters, "with the American, uprooted from his native usages, and confronted with the alien usages of a subtle and ancient society." "Maule's Well, or Henry James and the Relation of Morals to Manners," *In Defense of Reason* (New York, 1947), p. 312.

[2] W. M. Frohock, "Morals, Manners, and Scott Fitzgerald," *Southwest Review,* XL (Summer, 1955), 224.

[3] "Fitzgerald Plain," *The New Yorker,* February 3, 1951, p. 80.

When Carraway's voice introduces and concludes the action, Fitzgerald makes us conscious of the narrator, whose role may first be outlined by a comparison in which he acts the foil to Gatsby. We may begin with a difference which Fitzgerald would rightly have approved: Gatsby is rich, Nick relatively poor. Gatsby is alone, mysterious, obsessed; Nick makes friends easily, his life is ordinary, and he is quite sane. Gatsby is without conscience except perhaps where Daisy is concerned, and Nick subjects every act and motive to the scrutiny of a lively moral sense. Gatsby learns nothing in the course of the novel, or at least until his doom has been secured, for he decided too early what he wanted and strove for it with a determination which subordinated all other demands. Although Nick is thirty years old in the summer of 1922, the time of the novel, he is still an adolescent when he settles on Long Island, with an adolescent's memory of the war, and he comes to New York to enter the bond-selling business chiefly because other restless young men are doing the same thing. Nick has no purposes, he thinks of no powers to realize, and only very gradually, not until sometime in 1924, does he come to understand what his New York interlude has meant.

I cannot presume that this view of Carraway's part in the novel constitutes a revolutionary interpretation of *The Great Gatsby*. Arthur Mizener, whose analysis of *The Great Gatsby* has appeared in several forms and is undoubtedly the most widely distributed, approves Fitzgerald's choice of form and recognizes the structural importance of the first-person convention: "By means of this narrator he [Fitzgerald] was able to focus his story." [4] But the novel is the story of Gatsby, "a poor boy from the Middle West," and when Mr. Mizener classifies *The Great Gatsby* as a "tragic pastoral," it is Gatsby who illustrates the difference between the "simple virtue" of the West, and the "sophistication" and "corruption" of the East.[5] The moral distance between the two localities may be measured in more profound ways if we take Nick Carraway as our example and his sensibility and intelligence as the recognizable determinants which inform the story with its meaning. Such a reading of *The Great Gatsby* must also be compared, and at several points, with the interpretation of R. W. Stallman, who, in "Gatsby and the Hole in Time," characterizes Nick as a "defunct arch-priest" and regards the notion that Nick is to be seen as the "moral center of the book" as possible only to the "duped

---

[4] "F. Scott Fitzgerald: The Poet of Borrowed Time," *Critiques and Essays on Modern Fiction,* 295. Mr. Mizener, an acute reader of Fitzgerald, is well aware of Nick's moral involvement in the action of *The Great Gatsby*. I can hope to complement his analysis by a fullness of treatment he did not judge necessary.

[5] *Ibid.,* p. 296.

reader." [6] Fitzgerald's intention that we understand clearly what happens to Carraway may be appreciated in the first part of the first chapter. The novel's extraordinary economy requires, at least in its best parts, an attentive reading of detail, and since there are barely two pages in the first section, a close following of the text will not be intolerable.

Nick Carraway begins his story with the recollection that his father advised him to reserve his judgment of others because they may not have had the same "advantages." Nick's tolerance has made him the confidant of some and the victim of others, but to preserve his caution he has always reminded himself that "a sense of the fundamental decencies is parcelled out unequally at birth." Carraway's father has warned him about the difficulties of moral judgment, a difficulty originating in circumstances of origin and inheritance. But conduct, Nick observes, must be principled in some fashion. There is a "limit" to toleration. "Conduct may be founded on the hard rock or on the wet marshes, but after a certain point I don't care what it's founded on." That is, while it may be impossible to fix moral responsibility or to determine derelictions from that responsibility, Nick insists that action reveal some principle and that toleration does not permit indifference. His criticism of the standards and conduct of his Long Island friends has tired him, he concludes; he can wish the world "to stand at a sort of moral attention forever"; he wants no more "riotous" glimpses into the human heart. We should be too hasty if we condemned Nick for an unhealthy curiosity or for pompous self-righteousness. The tone of his narrative is never offensively positive, and we shall see that what may appear to be a peculiar form of pride is actually a serious kind of candor. Nick considers not only his friends, but himself as well. He tells us plainly what should interest us in his tale, and he introduces us to a period of his own life in which he is not entirely blameless and neutral. The quality of plainness, the device of direct revelation, has appeared to R. W. Stallman as the mask of the hypocrite, who is betrayed, symbolically, by his "irregular lawn." [7] To the contrary, Nick's irregularities of behavior, his carelessness, do not escape his judgment; he does not grow more confused but learns to see more clearly what Eastern society and morality are and how he has been corrupted by them.

Nick prepares us for his personal involvement in the action by his next words, when he reveals his own origins, or his reasons for thinking that he had "advantages." He came from a family of "prominent,

---

[6] *Modern Fiction Studies,* I (November, 1955), 7.
[7] *Ibid.*

well-to-do people" who have lived in "this Middle Western city for three generations." They have enjoyed commercial success, act together as a family, and regard the decisions and conduct of their relatives with grave concern. They have inherited the moral seriousness of their Scottish ancestors, sustain their business and social position as a manifestation of their moral superiority, and have passed down to their heirs a strong "sense of the fundamental decencies."

The narrator's part complicates the action. We are expected to realize that what we are told comes to us through his peculiar agency, and therefore—to complete an obvious matter—our knowledge of the narrator will establish the limits of our knowledge of the whole action. Fitzgerald understood these limitations and in the direct, economical way of *The Great Gatsby* engages the reader at once in the particular interests which the novel should arouse. Immediately after his introductory remarks, Carraway narrates his first visit to the Buchanan household, where he delivers an exact description of a moneyed and corrupt Eastern society in Daisy's despair and in Tom's adulteries.

Here Nick meets Jordan Baker, a professional tennis player who has succumbed to the ennui of the frantic search for novelty and excitement to which she and others of her post-war generation had devoted themselves. She is also a persistent and obvious liar, and Nick soon perceives this fault. Yet he is interested in her, though exactly how intimate they become is only suggested by a scene in which Jordan easily accepts Nick's first attentions. Her unconcern for any standards beyond those of a frank self-indulgence is evidence enough that the two have become lovers. This relationship is Nick's most personal involvement in the dissolution which Jordan represents, and the perception of his share in a common guilt comes with his initial revulsion to his summer's experience, directly after Myrtle Wilson's death. He is suddenly disgusted by the vicious and now violent life about him, but even in his new wisdom, his passion for Jordan has not been completely destroyed. In his last conversation with her, he can feel that he might be "making a mistake" by ending their affair and finally that he is "half in love with her." We learn most about them at this point in Jordan's accusation that Nick is a "bad driver." He is not the person she thought—not what he pretended to be—and she says, "It was careless of me to make such a wrong guess. I thought you were rather an honest, straightforward person. I thought it was your secret pride." Nick answers: "I'm thirty. I'm five years too old to lie to myself and call it honor." It was Nick's pride to feel that he could accept Jordan on her own terms, with her cynicism and her irresponsibility, and yet that he could escape the consequences of that acceptance. But what was subdued or ignored has now erupted, with Gatsby murdered and with Daisy and Tom exposed in their terrible selfishness. It can no longer be honorable for Nick to maintain the pretense that nothing serious is involved in his affair with Jordan. Nick was dishonest because he acted as though he brought no other standards of conduct to judge their liaison with than those which Jordan's hedonism impose; and it is now plain, in his disgust and self-recrimination, that Nick has in fact deceived Jordan. She accuses him of having thought of her all along as he does now, when he has given her up. She is right, of course, and Nick, who is (he tells us) the most honest man he knows, admits his twice-compounded duplicity, a duplicity analyzed in a similar way by R. W. Stallman. But he does not accept Nick's understanding of his personal responsibility. When Jordan "calls his bluff," as Stallman puts it, the effect is to make public Nick's own shame, so that, far from being "identified" with Jordan,[8] Nick is separated from her and from her society. He can no longer lie, and he leaves the East, without honor perhaps, but with a new-found vision of his own guilt.

There is another complication in Nick's discovery of his error. Even Jordan Baker, he says, came from the West. All the Westerners —Tom, Daisy, Gatsby, Jordan, and Nick—"possessed some deficiency in common which made us subtly unadaptable to Eastern life." Though the rest may have become more acclimated to the atmosphere of Eastern society than Nick, none is entirely at ease. None can rid himself of that "sense of the fundamental decencies," however attenuated it may have become, which their origins have given them. None can finally be comfortable in the hedonism cultivated by the Eastern representatives of his generation, or at least by those with money and enough intelligence to be disillusioned by the war. After his revulsion, Nick returns to the comparatively rigid morality of his ancestral West and to its embodiment in the manners of Western society. He alone of all the Westerners can return, since the others have suffered, apparently beyond any conceivable redemption, a moral degeneration brought on by their meeting with that form of Eastern society which developed during the twenties.

Nick makes another commitment to the life he at last rejects, a commitment that includes what we should ordinarily take to be his humiliating part in the affair between Gatsby and Daisy. Nick is used and knows it, but his attachment to Gatsby leads him to make another important discovery, however vague it may remain in some respects, about the nature of morality itself. We should ask: What does Nick think of Gatsby? And why? And again a passage at the beginning of the novel will reveal the essential information.

After Nick has explained that there must be limits to his toleration,

[8] *Ibid.,* p. 8

he excepts Gatsby from his general reaction, "Gatsby, who represented
everything for which I have an unaffected scorn." "There was something gorgeous about him, some heightened sensitivity to the promises
of life. . . ." Gatsby had "an extraordinary gift for hope, a romantic
readiness." Gatsby, Nick says, "turned out all right at the end," and
it was not he who drew Nick's scorn, but the "foul dust" which
"floated in the wake of his dreams." We learn gradually about Gatsby's
dream: about the events of his early life and his peculiar training,
about his obsession, about his impersonal—indeed, royal—view of his
own personality, about the reality which his vision of the perfect
life must have seemed to him. Now, the capacities which Nick admires
are the capacities of will: a tremendous energy to accomplish certain
purposes, and a self-imposed delusion which makes those purposes
meaningful. The delusion is the vision of Gatsby's life with Daisy,
and the purposes are his need for money and social position to make
himself worthy of her. Gatsby differs from the others of his time by
virtue of these capacities. Whereas the behavior of the Eastern rich,
the racketeers, and the Westerners who adopt Eastern ways is restricted
and debased by the selfish motives of personal and sensual gratifica-
tion, Gatsby acts for a good which he conceives, almost absurdly, as
being beyond personal interest. Gatsby's last heroism in protection of
the mistress of his dream confirms Nick's judgment. Gatsby does turn
out all right, while Tom and Daisy sit comfortably at their family
table, bound in their private safety. If Gatsby, as Nick says at the end,
"felt that he had lost the old warm world, paid a high price for living
too long with a single dream," his sacrifice has already been made and
his life consummated. He had found a way to live as men had once
lived, with a purpose and a meaning which transcended personal fate.

Nick accepts the probability that Gatsby himself realized the in-
sufficiency of his dream. The vision was only Gatsby's and his goal
only a personal one, if somehow ennobled, as Nick sees it, by Gatsby's
strength of will. Further, Gatsby is a fraud. The structure of appearance erected to impress Daisy is founded on some kind of illegal traffic
which only repels her, so that she is lost to Gatsby even before the
accident of Myrtle's death. Nor is Nick ever in any doubt that Gatsby
has valued only the tawdry and the vain. He is left at last with
Gatsby's morality, or rather Gatsby's capacity to live according to a
morality, his "romantic readiness." It is this ability which Nick feels
that he and the others lack, presumably because of historical circumstance.

That, at least, is what I take to be the meaning of the last words
of the novel, on the night when Nick left West Egg forever, and the
"inessential houses began to melt away until gradually I became
aware of the old island here that flowered once for Dutch sailors'

eyes—a fresh, green breast of the new world. Its vanished trees, the trees that had made way for Gatsby's house, had once pandered in whispers to the last and greatest of all human dreams. . . ." In Nick's day, I conclude, such dreams no longer correspond to any reality.[9] They present no real challenges, and only disillusion, even for a man like Gatsby, can ensue, if a lesser dream like Gatsby's is accepted. When Gatsby "picked out the green light at the end of Daisy's dock," Nick continues, "he did not know that it [his dream] was already behind him." A last contrast may now be made clear between Gatsby and Nick, Gatsby who thought he could remake the past and Nick who knew that it was irretrievably lost and that more than Gatsby's dream was gone with it.

Nick's discovery is that the power of will without the direction of intelligence is a destructive power, that there must be some real end beyond the satisfaction of private desire—however desire may be exalted—to justify the expenditure of life. But he believes too that, except for the anachronistic and fatal instance of Gatsby, the time when such ends could have existed is now done. We can only "beat on, boats against the current, borne back ceaselessly into the past."

Fitzgerald represents the past both as a loss and as a source of strength. It is the record of such deeds springing from such dedication as cannot now be expected, and in the Carraway family tradition, it confers a discipline and standards which, even as survivals of an old morality, may still produce better conduct than Nick witnesses on Long Island. Nick's honesty and his conception of a good existing beyond selfish ends may be only heirlooms, he realizes, honored for sentimental reasons, but they have been given a contemporary, limited reality in his own life. Nick includes his morality in his description of a graceless modern age and reduces his claims on it to the satisfaction of individual conscience. He has no real alternative—in the sense that it may be said to be available to other men—to the selfishness he condemns in Tom or Jordan. He does not speak authoritatively. But while his voice is subdued, it is never unsure. Nick's judgments are firm because he assumes that evil may be clearly enough determined. His hopes are modest because he regards the good only as a private, incommunicable possession. He can assert his criticism and judgment of Eastern society, including the revelation of his own guilt, but he affirms no morality of his own, accepting the circumstances of

[9] Edwin S. Fussell suggests that the dream of the Dutch sailors was also "unreal" and relies on the associations of the word *pandered* to develop this theme of the failure of romantic wonder, the quest for youth and success. "Fitzgerald's Brave New World," *ELH*, XIX (1952), 298. The interpretation may be allowed, but only, I think, if the old dream be regarded as the "last and greatest." Gatsby's dream was, to repeat, an illusion.

his birthright rather than affirming its permanent values. That Nick proposes to "save the world by regimenting it," [10] as R. W. Stallman has it, because he wants the world to be at a "sort of moral attention forever" is a reading which attributes this understandable reaction, this moral inertia, to a rigidity which Nick's private convictions could not support. Fitzgerald—so far as we can discern from the tenor of his narration—expects to meet no disagreement with his perception of evil, but assumes that he and his readers will all be perplexed to find a common good. This combination of conviction and diffidence produces the extraordinary contrast between the effects of cryptic description (as in Gatsby's youthful regimen) and of ideographic device (as in Dr. Ekleburg's eyes) and the quiet and deprecated role of the narrator.

Such an interpretation credits Fitzgerald with a moral seriousness which has, with reason, been challenged. With R. W. Stallman, W. S. Frohock finds Nick "short on moral perspective" [11] and Fitzgerald's style catching the "feeling of things" but combined with a "romantic inability to interpret them." [12] Edwin S. Fussell, on the other hand, defines the story of *The Great Gatsby* and other works as "the work of the imagination in the New World";[13] its failure to discover an objective for the romantic capacity is an American tragedy.[14] Failure, of course, attends Gatsby's career as inexorably as the current which sweeps the boats back into the past, but the failure must be experienced through Nick's moral sense, and his difficulties must be judged not as a lack of moral perspective but as the occasion for moral action of a peculiarly limited sort. Such a reading of Nick's role restores the emphasis which Fitzgerald gave to that moral judgment (developing awkwardly, it is true) which gives the novel its very form. And it may cast some light on the question of what Fitzgerald's early Catholic training may have meant to him:[15] a training which left him with the means to analyze and judge post-war American society even while he had lost the convictions which might have produced something more positive than Nick's retreat to the West.

The Great Gatsby is not a melodrama about Jay Gatsby, but a definition of the senses in which Nick understands the word "great." Its subject is an American morality. It is explored historically through the conflict between the surviving Puritan morality of the West and

[10] "Gatsby and the Hole in Time," p. 7.
[11] "Morals, Manners, and Scott Fitzgerald," p. 227.
[12] *Ibid.*, p. 228.
[13] "Fitzgerald's Brave New World," p. 291.
[14] *Ibid.*, p. 297.
[15] See the query by Professor H. W. Hausermann in *Modern Fiction Studies*, II, 2 (May, 1956), 81-82.

the post-war hedonism of the East; topically, through characteristic manifestations of American money values; formally and most significantly, through the personal history of a young American provincial whose moral intelligence is the proper source of our understanding and whose career, in the passage from innocence to revaluation, dramatizes the possibility and mode of a moral sanction in contemporary America.

Against *The Great Gatsby*

by Gary J. Scrimgeour

Since the Fitzgerald revival took shape, we have all tended to regard *The Great Gatsby* as the redemption for the manifest sins of Fitzgerald's other works. It is just good enough, just lyrical enough, just teachable-to-freshmen enough (and more than "American" enough) for unwary souls to call it a classic. Its superiority is seen in its craftsmanship, especially in a tighter structure that gives much greater depth and integrity to its content. It is usually difficult to evaluate the truth of claims that an author is both a fine technician and an intelligent moralist, but in this case Joseph Conrad's *Heart of Darkness* offers an appropriate measuring-stick. Conrad, as is well known, stood persistently firm in Fitzgerald's disorderly pantheon. There is evidence especially in *The Great Gatsby* that Fitzgerald's admiration extended as far as imitation, and the similarity between these two works enables us to challenge claims for Fitzgerald's intellectual and artistic merit by showing how much better Conrad could think and write.*

The most important of the similarities between the two novels is the use of the first-person narrator as a character in his own story.

"Against The Great Gatsby*" by Gary J. Scrimgeour. From* Criticism, *VIII (Winter, 1966), 75-86. Copyright © 1966 by Wayne State University Press, Reprinted by permission of the author and publisher.*

* This essay brings a new point of view and fresh material to a controversy raised by previous critics. Rather than expressing my agreements or disagreements in a series of footnotes, I refer the reader to the following articles: R. W. Stallman, "Gatsby and the Hole in Time," *Modern Fiction Studies*, I (Nov. 1955), 2-16; T. Hanzo, "The Theme and the Narrator of *The Great Gatsby*," *Modern Fiction Studies*, II (Winter, 1956-57), 183-190; J. Thale, "The Narrator as Hero," *Twentieth Century Literature*, III (July 1957), 69-73. On Conrad's influence on Fitzgerald see James E. Miller, *F. Scott Fitzgerald: His Art and His Technique* (New York, 1964), especially pp. 92-95, 106-113; R. W. Stallmann, "Conrad and *The Great Gatsby*," *Twentieth Century Literature*, I (April, 1955), 5-12; John Kuehl, "Scott Fitzgerald's Reading," *Princeton University Library Chronicle*, XXII (Winter, 1961), 58-59. Miller writes: "Probably the greatest influence on Fitzgerald during the gestation period of *The Great Gatsby* was Joseph Conrad" (p. 92). The parallels between *Heart of Darkness* and *The Great Gatsby* are sufficiently striking to suggest direct influence, but even if Conrad were not the source of Fitzgerald's technique, the Marlow stories would remain valid as a standard of comparison for the use of first-person narration.

In both novels a thoughtful man (Carraway, Marlow) recounts his moralized tale of the fate of an exceptional man (Gatsby, Kurtz). Their tales are essentially adventure stories. Both narrators are stirred by restlessness to seek exotic experience, encounter their "hero" by chance, become unwillingly intrigued by him, and are caught up in an intimacy which ends with the hero's death. Both are forced to pay tribute to their dead in the form of resounding lies (Marlow to Kurtz's fiancée; Carraway at the inquest), and then they retire for wound-licking and the later creation of their understated moralizations. Marlow and Carraway are alike in nature as well as function. Neither story would be about men possessed of absurd but enormous romantic dreams unless both narrators were of the kind of sensitivity that enabled them to see *la condition humaine* in the fates of irritating and egocentric individuals. Both feel a simultaneous repulsion and attraction for their heroes, dislike for their personality countered by admiration for their magnitude. Both men pretend to open-mindedness, modesty, and honesty. It is certain Marlow learns something from Kurtz's fate; it is claimed that Carraway learns from Gatsby's failure.

I give special emphasis to the use of the first-person narrator in the two novels for a particular reason. One forgets how recently we have come to see that Marlow is a character in the story he tells, rather than a translucent medium for transmitting a tale. In some novels the first-person narrator is merely a convenience in achieving selectivity, and in others at the opposite extreme the narrator himself is the object of our study. In *Heart of Darkness* both purposes are served; Marlow is both a technical device and part of the subject-matter. In *The Great Gatsby* the situation of Carraway is the same as that of Marlow, but I believe that Fitzgerald, never a great critical theorist, did not realize the dual nature of his narrator and therefore handled him very clumsily—and very revealingly.

When a narrator is also a character, with all that this implies of personality, individuality, and responsibility, we readers are forced to be more alert. We must question the accuracy of the narrator's account. When he makes judgments, we have to decide whether his special interests betray the truth and whether the meaning of each particular event and of the whole fable differs from the interpretation he offers. In *Heart of Darkness* Conrad is highly conscious of these problems and takes steps to solve them. Not all of the novel is in Marlow's words. He is presented and characterized by another narrator. He is given a setting, and he tells his story for an audience. He interrupts his own narrative several times, once to comment that "Of course in this you fellows see more than I could then. You see me, whom you know. . . ." By thus drawing attention to his existence as a character in the story he tells, he refuses to allow us to ignore his subjectivity, so that it becomes difficult to read *Heart of Darkness* without realizing that it is not just a fable about universals but also an interpreted personal experience.

Things are otherwise with *The Great Gatsby.* The entire novel is the narrator's written word, and with peril do we underestimate the significance of the change in manner from Marlow's oral delivery, full of hesitations, temporizings, and polished lack of polish, to the smooth veneer of Carraway's public, written narrative. It is quite legitimate to ask why Fitzgerald should follow Conrad closely in narrative technique except for those elements which warn us that the narrator may be giving us a truth which is anything but unvarnished. Why remove Conrad's surrogate audience and inset narrative? Why exchange the honest hesitancy of Marlow's manner for Carraway's literary imitation of charming spontaneity? Carraway is a disarmingly frank chap, and, as with most such fellows, his self-revelations are highly contrived. Is his opening characterization of himself as accurate as it is influential? During the narrative he tells us what to think of his actions, but should we judge by what he says or what he does? It is an obvious enough point, but it is exactly here that readers go astray and that Fitzgerald's artistic and ethical inferiority lie. Conrad knew that problems would arise and provided material to alert the reader. Fitzgerald promptly abandoned that material and led readers to follow Carraway's interpretation of events without realizing that there should be a difference, a gap, a huge gulf, between Carraway's and their conceptions of the affair.

Let us examine the relationship between the two novels more deeply. In *Heart of Darkness* the point of the use of a first-person narrator is that what has happened to the central figure is explained by what we see happen to the narrator; and, reciprocally, the weakness evident in the central figure reveals a similar but unsuspected flaw in the character of the narrator. Kurtz is presented to us at the moment when failure overwhelms him, and it is in the development of Marlow that we see the causes of Kurtz's defeat. Marlow feels and explains to us his awareness of the same decay that overcame Kurtz. The melodrama accompanying Kurtz's magnificence prevents its direct presentation, but it can be comprehended through the more life-size abilities and weaknesses of Marlow. In return, the fate of Kurtz reveals the peril of weaknesses which Marlow shares, and we thus realize that the same destruction could overcome the balanced, "normal" Marlow, and by corollary, any human being.

A very similar relationship exists between narrator and central figure in *The Great Gatsby,* but, unless Fitzgerald was much subtler than anyone has yet suggested, I do not think he realized it. While he tried to create a Marlovian narrator by asserting that Carraway has all of Marlow's desirable characteristics, his abandonment of the material which would allow an objective evaluation of his narrator's character shows that he understood neither the full purpose of Conrad's technique nor that Carraway's character is in fact very different from what Carraway claims it to be. Indeed Fitzgerald reveals a fault frequent in romantic writers, the inability to understand the true natures of the characters he created.

Take, for example, Gatsby himself, a character who usually and despite Carraway's warnings wins grudging admiration from readers. Like all romantic ideals, he is what personally we would not be so foolish as to imitate but nonetheless admire for its grandeur. It is refreshing to see, without Carraway's intervening intelligence, exactly to what sort of person we are giving our sympathy. Gatsby is a boor, a roughneck, a fraud, a criminal. His taste is vulgar, his behavior ostentatious, his love adolescent, his business dealings ruthless and dishonest. He is interested in people—most notably in Carraway himself —only when he wants to use them. His nice gestures stem from the fact that, as one character comments, "he doesn't want any trouble with *any*body." Like other paranoiacs, he lives in a childish tissue of lies and is unaware of the existence of an independent reality in which other people have separate existences. What lifts him above ordinary viciousness is the magnitude of his ambition and the glamor of his illusion. "Can't repeat the past?" he says to Carraway. "Why of course you can. . . ." To Gatsby, to repeat the past is to suppress unwanted elements of it and to select only nice things from which to make an uncontaminated present. Grand this defiance of reality may seem; silly it nonetheless is. Indeed it is no more than "a promise that the rock of the world was founded securely on a fairy's wing," and it crumbles as soon as it encounters reality in the form of Daisy. As long as his life is controlled by his own unattained desires, Gatsby's vision remains safe; he continually recreates the present in the light of his own needs. But as soon as Daisy's independent will enters the dream, Gatsby is forced to attach himself to the real world, to lose his freedom of action, and to pay the penalty for denying the past in having that past destroy the romantic present.

Gatsby's moral error is at least as clear as Kurtz's, and yet we give him our sympathy. Sneakingly we like Gatsby, while I defy anybody to *like* Kurtz. Partly this is because of Gatsby's adherence to the official American sexual code, the only moral code he does obey (whereas Kurtz has his native wife and indulges in "unspeakable rites"), but the major reason for the difference in our attitudes to the two men is the different reactions of Carraway and Marlow to their heroes' moral weaknesses. Where Marlow ends up loathing Kurtz, Carraway specifically tells us that he is not disgusted by Gatsby but by the mys-

terious "foul dust that floated in the wake of his dreams." Fitzgerald
provides many obscure but pretty metaphors to evoke Carraway's
ambiguous attitude to Gatsby's faults, and I think he is forced into
metaphor because only metaphor will conceal the fact that the story
as Carraway tells it is a paean to schizophrenia. Carraway is not deceived, of course, into admiring the superficialities of Gatsby's character and behavior; he represents everything for which Carraway
professes an "unaffected scorn." And yet at the same time something
makes Gatsby "exempt" from Carraway's reaction to the rest of the
world. Carraway tells us that Gatsby's great redeeming quality is his
"heightened sensitivity to the promises of life." Whether we criticize
or praise Carraway for being sufficiently young to believe that life
makes promises, we should notice at once that it is the promises—not
the realities—of life to which Gatsby is sensitive, and that Carraway
is in fact praising that very attempt to deny the past and reality whose
failure he is recounting.

This flaw in Carraway's moral vision is illuminating because it
shows that Gatsby stands in relationship to Carraway as Daisy stands
to Gatsby. Gatsby represents the promises of life with which the root-
less, twenty-nine year old, hazy-minded Carraway is as obsessed as is
Gatsby himself. It is important in this respect to notice how closely
Carraway's development is tied to Gatsby's and that, just as Kurtz's
career is paralleled up to a point by that of Marlow, so does Carraway's reflect Gatsby's. It is not simply that Carraway becomes emotionally involved in Gatsby's affairs but that his attitude towards his
own life is entirely dependent on his feelings about Gatsby. As one
small example from many, his most lyrical expression of the rapture
he feels for the East comes immediately after he has been convinced
of the genuineness of Gatsby's romantic history. More important, his
love affair with Jordan Baker is a second-hand impulse stirred by her
revelations of Gatsby's love for Daisy. These are Carraway's words:

> Unlike Gatsby and Tom Buchanan, I had no girl whose disembodied
> face floated along the dark cornices and blinding signs, and so I drew up
> the girl beside me, tightening my arms. Her wan, scornful mouth smiled,
> and so I drew her up again closer, this time to my face.

As though they were shadows of Gatsby's emotions, Carraway's feelings for the city and his love for Jordan both instantly collapse as
soon as Daisy's infidelity to Gatsby is apparent, and he returns to the
Mid-West, to what had previously seemed the "ragged edge of the
universe" but has now become a haven. Gatsby's defeat brings down
Carraway's dream as well.

In fact Gatsby himself is Carraway's romantic dream. The only
difference between the world that Carraway despises and the man he

admires is that Gatsby does things more spectacularly. In not seeing this, Carraway reveals that just like Gatsby he is willing to accept only those parts of reality which please him. He wants Gatsby to be different from the rest of the world; therefore Gatsby *is* different from the rest of the world. If we look at Carraway's behavior more closely, we may see that he shares others of Gatsby's failings, and that if Gatsby is no romantic hero, Carraway is even less the pleasant, anonymous, and highly principled character that he seems to be.

Were Carraway to characterize himself in a traditional phrase rather than metaphor, that phrase would be "man of principle." And yet his principles are challenged by the person who is presumably closest to him: Jordan Baker. Early in their relationship, Carraway and Jordan have a conversation which ends with Jordan saying, "I hate careless people. That's why I like you." After the sudden collapse of their affair, Jordan returns to this conversation in their last interview, when she accuses him of having thrown her over:

> "Oh, and do you remember"—she added—"a conversation we had once about driving a car?"
>
> "Why—not exactly."
>
> "You said a bad driver was only safe until she met another bad driver? Well, I met another bad driver, didn't I? I mean it was careless of me to make such a bad guess. I thought you were rather an honest, straightforward person. I thought it was your secret pride."
>
> "I'm thirty," I said. "I'm five years too old to lie to myself and call it honor."

Jordan is right about Carraway's character. The crisis of their affair reveals to her what she must have suspected before, that Carraway is neither as honest nor as high-principled as he might like to seem. It is interesting to note that she accuses him of the same "carelessness" that is the refrain in Carraway's attack on the Buchanans and the rest of the world. Her accusation suggests that at least in his dealings with her he has been as shabby as anyone else in East Egg.

And certainly his behavior with Jordan is no worse that the rest of his personal relationships, from the girl back home to Gatsby himself. Involved as he is with Daisy, Tom, Gatsby, and the Wilsons, he never acts well, just weakly. He fails to sense any obligation to avoid the flagrant dishonesty of his position and—far from feeling any qualms about playing either God or pander—he actually helps the others to continue activities which he later claims to regard as unworthy. His main principle is to say nothing. Most important is the final falsehood into which his loyalty to the dead Gatsby forces him. There is no intimation at all that at the inquest he feels his position of concealing the true facts to be in any way anomalous.

Where we might reasonably expect some explanation of his attitude, he dismisses the event with the comment that "all this part of it seemed remote and unessential." He simply prefers to conceal the truth rather than have the story "served up in racy pasquinade" and praises Mrs. Wilson's sister for "character" when she, "who might have said anything, didn't say a word." Is his behavior here, or even his attitude, superior to that of Tom, Daisy, Gatsby, or any other of the inhabitants of the ashland? Let us not be deceived by his condescension towards Wolfsheim's "gonnegtions" or his smugness about people who cheat at golf.

Another significant episode occurs near the end of the novel, when he encounters Tom for the last time. At first he avoids him because he is convinced that Tom was the cause of Gatsby's death. He says that he could neither forgive nor like Tom and Daisy because of their talent for "smashing up things" and retreating into "their vast carelessness," a firm moral judgment in words which we might expect from a principled man. But let us look at the act that follows:

> I shook hands with him; it seemed silly not to, for I felt suddenly as though I were talking to a child. Then he went into the jewelry store to buy a pearl necklace—or perhaps only a pair of cuff-buttons—rid of my provincial squeamishness forever.

While shaking hands with Tom may be an urbane gesture to avoid embarrassment, it is certainly not honest either to Tom or to Carraway's principles, and to turn from recognition of the villainy of Tom's behavior to dismissal of it as the behavior of a child is not a sign of moral profundity or consistency. Carraway's honesty is a matter not of principle, but of convenience. (Whether the reader likes or dislikes men of principle is irrelevant—we are concerned only with Carraway's claims to be one.)

One could attack Carraway's nature further; to one who dislikes him, the opening and closing pages of the novel are a lexicon of vanity. But the key issue is undoubtedly his honesty, because that provides the basis of the reader's reaction to the novel. It is here that he contrasts most strongly with Conrad's Marlow. For example, both Marlow and Carraway are reticent about many important matters, but when Marlow refuses to linger on a subject (such as the rites in which Kurtz participates) it is because enough has already been said; more would be too much. Carraway's reticences, however, verge on falsehood. Instead of stopping short with just the right impression, they often succeed in giving the wrong impression. The lie that Carraway acquiesces in at the inquest and the complaisance he reveals in finally shaking hands with Tom have as their motive no nobler desire than to let sleeping dogs lie, whereas Marlow, who finds himself pushed at the end of *Heart of Darkness* into an agonizing untruth, lies because the truth would be infinitely more damaging and useless. The truth about Mrs. Wilson's death could be damaging, but it is more likely to be simply incommoding. We have, in any case, no sign from Carraway that he even considered the problem.

Honesty can in the end be based only on some kind of powerful drive, and this is something that Carraway does not possess. The real nature of his principles appears if we contrast his own estimate of his integrity with a similar statement by Marlow. Long after the events which wrapped him inextricably in falsehood, Carraway writes, "Everyone suspects himself of at least one of the cardinal virtues, and this is mine: I am one of the few honest people that I have ever known." Marlow, on the occasion not of a falsehood but of a minor false impression, says:

> You know I hate, detest and can't bear a lie, not because I am straighter than the rest of us, but simply because it appalls me. There is a taint of death, a flavor of mortality in lies—which is exactly what I hate and detest in the world—what I want to forget. It makes me miserable and sick, like biting something rotten would do. Temperament, I suppose.

The difference between Marlow's and Carraway's words is the difference between a man who cannot deny reality and a man who cannot face it. Both men feel deeply, but Marlow, at the cost of real pain, has to push forward until he understands the meaning of what he feels, until he is honest with himself, whereas Carraway stops short with whatever feeling he can conveniently bear, dreading what further effort might uncover. Both men record as much as they understand, but Marlow's honesty forces him to a much deeper understanding than Carraway achieves. To Marlow, feeling is part of the process that creates understanding, and honesty is his strongest feeling; to Carraway, feeling is the end product of experience, and honesty a matter for self-congratulation.

If the reader cannot accept Carraway's statements at face value, then the integrity of the technique of the novel is called in question. Rather than accepting what Carraway claims to be the effect of the events on his nature, the reader must stand further off and examine Carraway's development as though he were any other character, in which case a second vital weakness becomes obvious. Again like Gatsby, he never realizes the truth about himself, and despite the lesson of Gatsby's fate he fails to come to self-knowledge. There is a curious use of the conditional in Carraway's introduction to his story. He writes, "If personality is an unbroken series of successful gestures, then there was something gorgeous about [Gatsby], some heightened sensitivity to the promises of life." The reason for Carraway's hesitancy over a matter that should present no problem is that he himself is trying to construct a personality out of a series of gestures such as the "clean break" with Jordan or the final handshake with Tom, behavior which results from his inability to decide what he should be doing or why he should be doing it. He is a moral eunuch, ineffectual in any real human situation that involves more than a reflex action determined by social pattern or the desire to avoid trouble with "*any*body." At one stage Carraway senses that something is wrong and suggests that Tom, Gatsby, Daisy, Jordan, and he all "possessed some deficiency in common," but he fails to see that the deficiency is the hollowness in their moral natures that leaves them prey to self-deception and "carelessness."

Consequently Carraway's distinctivness as a character is that he fails to learn anything from his story, that he can continue to blind himself even after his privileged overview of Gatsby's fate. The defeat evident in his disillusionment is followed not by progress but by retreat. He returns not only to his safe environment in the Mid-West but also to the same attitudes from which he started. One cannot praise him for being disillusioned with the ashland life of the East. For him to be disillusioned with values that are, after all, transparently unworthy, is not as remarkable as the fact that he remains enamored of the person who represents those values in their most brilliant and tempting form. He refuses to admit that his alliance with Gatsby, his admiration for the man, results from their sharing the same weakness. Writing when he has had time to deliberate on Gatsby's fate, he says, "Only Gatsby . . . was exempt from my reaction—Gatsby, who represented everything for which I have an unaffected scorn." This is precisely the attitude which he held long before, at the height of his infatuation with Gatsby's dream. He has learned nothing. His failure to come to any self-knowledge makes him like the person who blames the stone for stubbing his toe. It seems inevitable that he will repeat the same mistakes as soon as the feeling that "temporarily closed out my interest in the abortive sorrows and short-winded elations of men" has departed. The world will not, despite his wishes, remain "at a sort of moral attention forever."

Because of the weakness of Carraway's character, the meaning of *The Great Gatsby* is much blacker than that of *Heart of Darkness*. In the latter Marlow progresses through his encounter with Kurtz to a greater self-knowledge; and even if we consider self-knowledge a pitiful reward to snatch from life, we must still admit that it has a positive value and that the gloom of the story is not unrelieved. Such cautious optimism is apparent only if we can see first that the narrator of *Heart of Darkness* is a reliable purveyor of truth, and second that he has come to greater self-knowledge. It is to the end of emphasizing these qualities that Conrad fashions the structure of the novel. The beginning of the work and the interruptions in Marlow's narrative have the purpose of reminding us at key points that the story is being refracted through Marlow's mind and that he is a character whose reactions are as important as his tale. The most emphasized of Marlow's qualities are his self-knowledge (we recall his Buddha-like pose) and the stress of his desire to fight his way through the material of his experience to reveal the truth. We can accept Marlow's recounting of the events only if we believe that, both as narrator and as person, his judgment is to be respected, and Conrad takes some of the novel out of Marlow's hands for exactly this purpose.

But we have seen that it is just here that Fitzgerald makes a major change in the structure of *The Great Gatsby*. There is little doubt that we are intended to see Carraway both as a reliable narrator and as a character learning from experience, but because we see only his version of the events and of his character, an objective evaluation is difficult. When we do attempt to be objective, we find that we have to impugn Carraway's honesty as a narrator and his self-awareness as a person. In this way Fitzgerald's change in technique makes *The Great Gatsby* a much more pessimistic novel than *Heart of Darkness*. If the story means (as Fitzgerald probably intended) that Gatsby's romantic dream is magnificent and Carraway's change a growth, then we have a somber but reasonably constructive view of life. But if our narrator turns out to be corrupt, if our Adam is much less innocent than we suspected, then despair replaces elegy. Had Carraway been defeated by the impersonal forces of an evil world in which he was an ineffectual innocent, his very existence—temporary or not—would lighten the picture. But his defeat is caused by something that lies within himself: his own lack of fibre, his own willingness to deny reality, his own substitution of dreams for knowledge of self and the world, his own sharing in the very vices of which his fellow men stand accused.

The irony produced by a comparison with the superficially gloomier *Heart of Darkness* is the realization that while Marlow sees the events as typical and Carraway as crucial, in effect they are crucial for Marlow and typical for Carraway. Where Marlow gains an expansiveness of outlook from his experiences, we find Carraway saying that "life is much more successfully looked at from a single window, after all," surely a supreme expression of the ethical vacuity which brought about his sufferings in the first place. If the one person who had both the talent and the opportunity to realize his own weaknesses remains unchanged, then we have a world of despair. Perhaps in this light the final image of the novel gains a new felicitousness: "So we beat on, boats against the current, borne back ceaselessly into the past."

It is usually considered that Fitzgerald intended *The Great Gatsby* to warn us against the attempt to deny reality. My interpretation of the novel goes further to suggest that unwittingly, through careless technique and cloudy thinking, Fitzgerald in fact created a novel which says that it is impossible for us to face reality. One would like to think that Fitzgerald knew what he was doing, that in the opening pages he intended Carraway's priggishness and enervation to warn the reader against the narrator. Certainly there is enough evidence in the novel to support such a view, which can no more be completely disproven than can similar readings of *Moll Flanders* and *Gulliver's Travels*, but before we accept it we have to answer two questions: was the young Fitzgerald capable of such ironic perception, which would involve an extraordinarily complex attitude not just to his characters but to his readers and to himself as writer and individual? and if so, why did he choose deliberately not to make the irony clearer to the reader, especially with the example of Conrad in front of him? My own belief is that Fitzgerald achieved something other than he intended. Knowing that he always had difficulty in distinguishing himself from his characters (and admitted to being even Gatsby!), we can legitimately suspect that Carraway's failure is Fitzgerald's failure, and that Fitzgerald himself was chronically unaware of the dangers of romanticism. If Daisy is Gatsby's dream, and Gatsby is Carraway's dream, one suspects that Carraway is Fitzgerald's dream.

Much of *The Great Gatsby* is of course brilliant, and its historical position as one of the earliest American novels to attempt twentieth-century techniques guarantees it a major position in our literary hierarchy. But it is usually praised for the wrong reasons, and we should take care that Fitzgerald does not become our dream, as the recent spate of biographies and articles might suggest. The character of Carraway as Fitzgerald saw it, the innocent Adam in the school of hard knocks, appeals to our liking for sentimental pessimism; critics and teachers can overvalue romanticism as much as authors, and thus damage our literary tradition by mistaking delicate perceptions for sound thinking. Unless we wish to teach what Fitzgerald intended rather than what he wrote, unless we prefer an attractive exterior to an honest interior, unless we cherish a novel because we think it says the things we want to hear, then we should be very precise about the value of what the novel actually says. Ultimately, to withdraw our sympathy from Carraway, even to lower our estimation of Fitzgerald's skill, is not to depreciate but to change the worth of *The Great Gatsby*. It may serve to teach both readers and writers that careful technique is worth more to a novel than verbal brilliance, and that honest, hard thinking is more profitable than the most sensitive evocation of sympathy. We may no longer be able to read it as a description of the fate that awaits American innocence, but we can see it as a record of the worse dangers that confront American sentimentality.

Dream, Design, and Interpretation
in *The Great Gatsby*

by David L. Minter

If thou didst ever hold me in thy heart,
Absent thee from felicity awhile,
And in this harsh world draw thy breath in pain,
To tell my story.
William Shakespeare, Hamlet

There is, as Kenneth Burke once noted, "a radical difference . . . between building a house and writing a poem about building a house." [1] Like Hawthorne's *The Blithedale Romance* and Faulkner's *Absalom, Absalom!*, Fitzgerald's *The Great Gatsby* is structured by the juxtaposition of men engaged in these radically different pursuits. On one side there is Jay Gatsby, who is a builder as well as a dreamer; on the other, there is Nick Carraway, who is a narrator as well as a spectator. Whereas Gatsby deliberately dedicates himself to realizing his "incorruptible dream," to building according to "the beautiful circuit and subterfuge" of his thought and his desire, Carraway deliberately dedicates himself not only to observing Gatsby's action but to telling Gatsby's story.[2]

The Great Gatsby is permeated with corruption and contains, in the valley of ashes, Fitzgerald's starkest image of the new world as waste land, yet it is not in the end simply a grim story. Jay Gatsby's "incorruptible" version of the "last and greatest of all human dreams"— the dream of building a new and perfect life in a new and perfect

"Dream, Design, and Interpretation in The Great Gatsby*" by David L. Minter. This is a hitherto unpublished essay, printed in this volume by permission of the author.*

[1] Quoted in Stanley Edgar Hyman, *The Armed Vision* (rev. ed., New York, 1959), p. 333.

[2] *The Great Gatsby* (New York, 1925), p. 155. All page references in the text are to this edition. Henry James, *The Art of the Novel: Critical Prefaces*, ed. R. P. Blackmur (New York, 1946), pp. 31-32.

world—serves, as several critics have noted, to relieve the novel's grim-
ness, to recast its bleakness.[3] Gatsby's action—his building, both as
activity and as artifact—ends, however, in "huge incoherent failure,"
not in success (181). It serves accordingly rather to make relief possible
than in itself to represent relief. The whole of Gatsby's story, including
both his dream and his absurd plan for realizing it—his plan for pro-
curing a fortune, a mansion, and a bride—is redeemed from corruption
and waste, from failure and absurdity only through Nick Carraway's
effort imaginatively to interpret and render it. The first four paragraphs of the novel prepare us for the form the novel's unfolding is to
take. In the first three paragraphs, the narrator, Nick Carraway, introduces himself; in the fourth he introduces the subject of his narrative,
Jay Gatsby. Carraway's small cottage on the edge of Gatsby's spacious
estate suggests the role he is to play within the novel: the role of observer and spectator, critic and interpreter of a scene and an action
dominated by Gatsby.

Gatsby represents, Carraway tells us, "everything for which I have an
unaffected scorn." Yet, because he has found in Gatsby "some heightened sensitivity to the promises of life"—"a romantic readiness"—and
because of the curious way in which Gatsby "turned out . . . at the
end," Carraway has not been able not to do Gatsby. Having watched
Gatsby pursue "his dream" with "unwavering devotion," Carraway
knows that Gatsby has lived in faith that man can shape his life at will,
compelling it to yield the beauty he seeks and the meaning he needs
(2, 110). Carraway accordingly knows that Gatsby has become what he
has become through "his extraordinary gift for hope"—his extraordinary faith that through devoted action he not only can shape the future
but can "fix" the "terrible mistake" that mars the past (2, 111, 131).
Moved as he is by faith in observing closely and "reserving judgments,"
Carraway is drawn to seek purpose in the "purposeless splendor" and
meaning in the problematic fate that define Gatsby's life (1, 79). Unlike Gatsby's faith, which leaves him vulnerable to destruction (see
137), Carraway's faith renders him vulnerable to despair: to loss of "interest in the abortive sorrows and short-winded elations of men" and
loss of faith in the effort "to save . . . fragment[s]" of "dead dream[s]"
(2, 153, 135). If, in Gatsby, Fitzgerald dramatizes the peculiar beauty
and vulnerability of one dedicated to actualizing dreams, in Carraway
he dramatizes the peculiar beauty and vulnerability of one dedicated
to finding meaning in the "undefined consequence" of an action (64).

Behind Gatsby there is a history of dislocation and alienation, the
attendants, as it were, of the experience of immigration, and thus of

---

[3] See pp. 155, 182. See Marius Bewley, "Scott Fitzgerald's Criticism of America,"
Sewanee Review, LXII (1954), 223-246; and Edwin Fussell, "Fitzgerald's Brave New
World," *English Literary History*, XIX (1952), 291-306.

the very process of Americanization.[4] But behind him there also is an imagined history. On one side, he is James Gatz, the son of "shiftless and unsuccessful farm people." On the other, he is Jay Gatsby, the child of "his Platonic conception of himself," the heir to a history almost wholly "invented." Unable in the presence of abundance, of mansions in the town and yachts upon the lake, to accept dislocation and deprivation, his imagination has created an identity, a "conception," to which he remains "faithful to the end" (98-99).

James Gatz's attempt to become Jay Gatsby, his attempt to live out of his invented history, entails an attempt to realize his "unutterable" dream (112). Given his world, his dream, despite its "gaudiness," is necessary. At times its vitality almost overwhelms him, almost reduces him to a mere embodiment of its impulse; and at times he almost fatally betrays it by making devotion to it take the form of service to a beauty that is "vast, vulgar, and meretricious" (98-99). From outset to end, he just misses "being absurd." [5] Yet both his conception of himself and his dream survive everything. To its curiously actual yet unreal world, Gatsby's dream comes as "a deathless song"; in its own way it is so "absolutely real" that it changes everything it touches "into something significant, elemental, and profound" (97, 46-47). Though altogether unactual, it is its world's primary source of positive good, its primary hope of overcoming the "foul dust" and the "valley of ashes" (2, 23).

Before it is finally rendered "incorruptible," however, Gatsby's particular version of "the last and greatest of all human dreams" becomes a "dead dream" and leads to "grotesque" "nightmare" (155, 182, 135, 164). And it does so because, in the design through which Gatsby attempts to actualize it, it is wed to "perishable breath" and mortal mansion. In entering the round world of time-space, it falls victim to the "accidental" and ends in "holocaust" (112, 162-163).

In its earliest recorded form, Gatsby's effort to express "his unutterable visions" takes the form of a "schedule" (a direct descendant of Benjamin Franklin's) copied on a flyleaf of "a ragged old copy of a book called *Hopalong Cassidy*." The schedule itself is intended to enforce industry and frugality, to foster physical, mental, and moral growth, and to encourage development of social graces and personal cleanliness—"No wasting time" / "No more smoking or chewing" / "Bath every other day" / "Practice elocution, poise and how to attain it" (112, 174). Later, goaded by loss of Daisy—to whom he has "felt himself married"—and by knowledge that the "terrible mistake" of her marriage with the wealthy Tom Buchanan is a result of his own

---

[4] See Oscar Handlin, *The Uprooted* (New York, 1951), pp. 4-5 and *passim*.

[5] See p. 48. Note that the quoted phrase refers specifically to Gatsby's voice, and cf. p. 174, where we learn that Gatsby's preparation for translating his dream into design includes practicing "elocution."

poverty, Gatsby turns his dream into a design that dictates a precise course of action. On one side, he will pursue "his phantom millions" —he will accumulate a prodigious fortune and procure a colossal mansion. On the other, he will pursue Daisy, to whom, as an embodiment of ideal beauty, he commits himself as "to the following of a grail" (131, 149).

Although it culminates in his own death, Gatsby's effort to turn dream to design and design to actuality provides the key to understanding his story. When Carraway first realizes that Gatsby's mansion is situated across the bay from Daisy's home, not by "strange coincidence," but by design, the whole of Gatsby's life begins to take form and to demand interpretation anew. "He came alive to me," Carraway says, "delivered suddenly from the womb of his purposeless splendor" (79).

The "romantic speculation" and "bizarre accusations" that Gatsby evokes from all sides represent responses to the rich mystery, the problematic ambience, in which he moves (44, 65). Gatsby takes "satisfaction" in these "legends" and "inventions"—reports, for instance, that he is a murderer, a German spy, a gangster, a nephew of Von Hindenburg, and a nephew or cousin of Kaiser Wilhelm—(44, 61, 33)—not simply because he prizes notoriety, but because he longs to be interpreted (98; cf. 67). What seems to Nick Carraway, who doesn't "like mysteries," [6] most to demand interpretation, however, is that Gatsby's design itself ends in ironic failure: that Gatsby's effort to right the moment of affront at the door of Daisy's "beautiful house" leads to more humiliating defeat at the more vulgar hands of Tom Buchanan; that Gatsby's effort to establish a grand mansion ends with an "empty" house that speaks only of "huge incoherent failure"; and that Gatsby's effort to have Daisy in order that she may reign as queen in his mansion ends not merely in unsuccess but in his death at the hands of a confused and outraged stranger (148, 181).

Nick Carraway's interpretation of Gatsby's fate involves more, however, than an inquiry into what went wrong in Gatsby's plan. In all Gatsby says and does, despite "his appalling sentimentality," there is an echo of "an elusive rhythm, a fragment of lost words" heard long ago. What accordingly is required of Carraway is that he define what lies behind Gatsby's design; and it is with this, as we shall see, that Carraway ends. Gatsby's sentimentality and silence together represent the residue of a dream for which his design is not an adequate correlative. Although it becomes "his ancestral home," although it corresponds to his invented history and is itself the work of a failed "plan to Found a Family," Gatsby's colossal mansion is not in itself com-

[6] See p. 72. Note that Carraway is extremely fastidious; he likes "to leave things in order" (p. 178).

mensurate with his needs. Similarly, despite the vitality of Gatsby's vision of her, Daisy remains, or at least again becomes, a curiously beautiful fraud of a hopelessly corrupt world. Only in Carraway's interpretation is the fullness of Gatsby's dream recovered (112, 154, 89).

Carraway's effort to interpret Gatsby is for the most part rather simple. In some moments he simply discredits what is false: he explodes "wild rumors" and clears away "misconceptions," just as, before leaving the mansion for the last time, he erases "an obscene word" that some unknown boy has scrawled on its white steps (102, 181). In other moments he records what he has directly observed or reports, either directly or indirectly, what he has heard or been told. In his most characteristic moments, however, he redeems failed action by endowing it with narrative order. The first party Gatsby gives on the "blue gardens" and grounds of his glowing mansion is rich in sound and color: while the orchestra plays "yellow cocktail music," the air comes "alive with chatter and laughter" that strain to become an "opera" (39-40; cf. 82). The "few [invited] guests" mingle with strangers who simply come, and together they become a "sea-change of faces" in search of the host no one knows (40-41; cf. 45). For a moment, when Gatsby first appears, the scene becomes what it is all along striving to be: it becomes "something significant, elemental, and profound." But the moment is fleeting. Order promptly gives way to "dissension" and ends in the "violent confusion" of "harsh, discordant din" (47, 52, 54). Only when Carraway glances "back" does Gatsby's failed party become something more than a weird collection of strangers and curiosity-seekers. Indeed, Gatsby himself survives the confused "sound of his still glowing garden" and overcomes the "sudden emptiness" of his mansion only because Carraway sees and renders him standing under a "wafer of a moon." Only in Carraway's narrative is Gatsby able paradoxically to stand at once in "complete isolation" and as a perfect "figure of the host" (56).

Finally, however, especially in recounting Gatsby's past and in reconstructing Gatsby's death, Carraway is forced, before he can give narrative form to Gatsby's story, to become, first, a detective, and then, an imaginative interpreter. The only adequate image of the "unquiet darkness" of Gatsby's world, the only adequate measure of the deep desolation that moves Carraway to assume his final interpretive stance, is the "desolate" "valley of ashes"—the "fantastic farm where ashes grow like wheat into ridges and hills and grotesque gardens; where ashes take the forms of houses and chimneys and rising smoke and, finally, with a transcendent effort, of men who move dimly and already crumbling through the powdery air" (22-23). Above this radically mortal world, in which the mixed motion of time carelessly changes all that men do and all that they are, there brood the grotesque, faded eyes of Doctor T. J. Eckleburg, just as, above the "waste land" of Gatsby's world there brood the eyes of Nick Carraway (23-24).[7] Unlike that of its synecdoche, however, the juxtaposition that defines the structure of the novel is neither specious nor sterile. In contrast to the soiled words and corrupted motives of the advertisement, Carraway's vision participates in the same "creative passion" we see in Gatsby's action. In the interim—"In the meantime," the "In between time"—world of *The Great Gatsby*, Carraway's interpreting vision is all we have (97). It is not to be confused, as George Wilson confuses Eckleburg's "persistent stare" (see 24, 160), with divine vision, but it does arrange and deepen, recapture and relate.

It is in his most fully interpretive moments—when he accepts the burden of imaginative reconstruction, when, in short, he plays the role Fitzgerald planned for Cecilia in his unfinished novel, *The Last Tycoon*—that Carraway most clearly functions as a deputy of the artist.[8] Only in such a moment, moreover—that is, only when he is presenting the events of the day following Tom Buchanan's effectual defeat of Gatsby and Daisy's accidental killing, with Gatsby's car, of Tom's mistress, in picturing Gatsby waiting for a call from Daisy, a call that could revive hope for his miscarried design—is Carraway able to attribute to Gatsby something approaching tragic illumination.

> No telephone message arrived. . . . I have an idea that Gatsby himself didn't believe it would come, and perhaps he no longer cared. If that was true he must have felt that he had lost the old warm world, paid a high price for living too long with a single dream. He must have looked up at an unfamiliar sky through frightening leaves and shivered as he found what a grotesque thing a rose is and how raw the sunlight was upon the scarcely created grass. A new world, material without being real, where poor ghosts, breathing dreams like air, drifted fortuitously about . . . [sic] like that ashen, fantastic figure gliding toward him through the amorphous trees (162).

When the ashen figure has come and killed the drifting ghost, when the holocaust is complete, all that remains is for Carraway to show why, despite all that is maudlin about him and despite the end with which he meets, Gatsby is worth more than the whole of the "rotten" world that destroys him (154).

The "creative passion" lying behind Carraway's effort to clear up each "tremendous detail" of Gatsby's life and fate enables him finally

---

[7] See Milton Hindus, "The Eyes of Dr. T. J. Eckleburg," *Boston University Studies in English*, III (1957), 22-31.

[8] See Thomas Hanzo, "The Theme and the Narrator of *The Great Gatsby*," *Modern Fiction Studies*, III (1956-1957), 183-190.

to render Gatsby's dream "incorruptible" (97, 129, 155). Carraway delivers Gatsby from mere "notoriety" and "wild rumors"; he completes him and makes him great. In themselves Gatsby's bizarre parties, his failed efforts to establish community, remain spectacular yet incoherent anthologies of celebrities and outcasts. In themselves the characteristically hidden scenes in which Gatsby approaches Daisy and seems to near realization of his design know no consummation (98, 102). In Carraway's narration, however, through imaginative translation, the man who in life has been left in "complete isolation" becomes the perfect figure of the host, and the mansion that through action has become a splendid mausoleum becomes again a mansion, its temporary inhabitant's true "ancestral home" (56, 154).

Carraway's triumph derives from his ability to stand both "within and without" the action he narrates—his ability to be a participant yet a "watcher in the darkening streets"—his ability to give himself, like James's wondering dawdlers, to always "looking up and wondering . . . simultaneously enchanted and repelled by the inexhaustible variety of life" (36), his ability, in fine, not only in observing to wonder but, through narrating, to cause another to wonder.[9] By suffering within, by understanding and relating the whole of what he sees not simply to his own life, nor merely to his country's history, but to all human endeavor, Carraway brings rich order to Gatsby's story. Having enabled Gatsby to stand under a "wafer of a moon" on the white steps of his mansion, overlooking "blue" grounds and "glowing garden," as a veritable icon "of the host" (56, 182; cf. 154), Carraway moves on to become a lyric poet. The "valley of ashes" and "the inessential houses" of the Sound together "melt away" until the valley of ashes and the green breast of the new world are coherently related and Gatsby's story (to borrow and reverse the phrase Gatsby himself has used in dismissing any possible love between Tom and Daisy) becomes not in the least "just personal" (23, 182, 152). We accordingly see behind Gatsby's dream an old vision and hear behind his voice "a fragment of lost words" heard long ago; we become aware that "the old island" once had been the "fresh, green breast of the new world," and that the "vanished trees, the trees that had made way for Gatsby's house, had once pandered in whispers to the last and greatest of all human dreams." In response to "something commensurate to his capacity for wonder," poised on the edge of a vast, empty continent of an open and new world, confident in all innocence, believing "in the green light, the orgiastic future" of perfection, man then had dared to respond, as Gatsby later was to respond, with wonder at the distance he had come and with faith that he now would live his dream (112,

[9] See James, p. 254.

182). Thus near to success, thus invited and enticed with pandered whispers by his world, he had dared to move beyond dreaming his dream to an attempt to live it. Because of the beauty of his dream and the heroism of his effort to move beyond it, Gatsby can be made great. Yet, because he has so dared only to see the vanishing trees give way, not to a city of man, but to a valley of ashes, not to the marriage and mansion envisaged, but to "huge incoherent failure" (181), he can be made great only through reconstituting interpretation, reordering art.

Theme and Texture in *The Great Gatsby*

by *W. J. Harvey*

Criticism of *The Great Gatsby,* when it has not been sidetracked into biography or reminiscence of the Jazz Age, has tended to concentrate on two issues. The first of these has been concerned with the moral seriousness of the book, with what answer, if any, can be given to the hostile critic of whom John Farelly, writing in *Scrutiny,* is a good example:

> I want to suggest that there is an emptiness in his work that makes "convincing analysis" honestly difficult, but leaves a hollow space where critics can create their own substitute Fitzgerald. And I should probe for that hollow space in what we call the *centre* of a writer's work—that around which and with reference to which he organizes his experiences; in short, his values.[1]

Closely related to this is the problem of what status we should allow Gatsby himself; in particular, we may note the attempt to see him as a mythic character and the novel as the expression of some deep-rooted and recurrent "American Dream." [2]

The first of these questions has been exhaustively debated and if neither side has much shaken the other's conviction, the issues are at least clearly defined; while anyone who is not an American will feel a natural diffidence about expressing any opinion on the second topic. In fact, what immediately impresses itself upon most readers—especially if they have come to *The Great Gatsby* after reading Fitzgerald's earlier novels—is not moral theme or national archetype but something much simpler, something so obvious, perhaps, that it has received remarkably little close critical attention. I mean the astonishing accession of technical power and skill. Less pretentious than his earlier work, *The Great Gatsby* achieves much more; in it Fitzgerald discovers not

---

"Theme and Texture in The Great Gatsby*" by W. J. Harvey. From* English Studies, *XXXVIII (1957), 12-20. Copyright © 1957 by Swets and Zeitlinger. Reprinted by permission of* English Studies.

[1] John Farelly, "Scott Fitzgerald: Another View," *Scrutiny,* XVIII (June, 1952).

[2] For example, Edwin S. Fussell, "Fitzgerald's Brave New World," *English Literary History,* 19 (December, 1952).

only his true subject but a completely adequate form. To say this, no doubt, is to say also that he has attained a maturity that transcends the merely aesthetic, that reveals itself also in the moral implications of the fable.

Nearly every critic of *The Great Gatsby* has stressed the tremendous structural importance of the narrator, Nick Carraway, the character through whom Fitzgerald is able to achieve that aesthetic distance from his own experience necessary for firmness of control and clarity of perception, through whom he can express that delicately poised ambiguity of moral vision, the sense of being "within and without, simultaneously enchanted and repelled by the inexhaustible variety of life" out of which insight into the truth of things must grow. William Troy has summed it up neatly and concisely:

> In the earlier books author and hero tended to melt into one another because there was no internal principle of differentiation by which they might be separated; they respired in the same climate, emotional and moral; they were tarred with the same brush. But in *Gatsby* is achieved a dissociation, by which Fitzgerald was able to isolate one part of himself, the spectatorial or esthetic, and also the more intelligent and responsible, in the person of the ordinary but quite sensible narrator, from another part of himself, the dream-ridden romantic adolescent from St. Paul and Princeton, in the person of the legendary Jay Gatsby.[3]

Again, most critics of the novel have amply demonstrated its economy, the clarity of its narrative outline and the forceful, unbroken drive of it forward from the first page to the last, an impetus which incorporates, and even gains momentum from, the cunningly interpolated flashbacks. Many critics have expanded and expounded the significance of the major symbolic structures of the book; indeed, to insist upon its legendary nature is to insist upon these. What more, then, can be said about the mastery of Fitzgerald's technique; what aspect of it has received less than its fair share of attention?

I should like, quite simply, to discuss the language of the book. Here we find, co-existing with economy, clarity and force, an extreme density of texture. It is this which ultimately gives richness and depth to the novel, this without which the larger symbols would lose their power of reverberating in the reader's mind and the major themes of the book would seem intellectual or emotional gestures, without the pressure of felt and imaginatively experienced life behind them.

We may best begin with a fairly detailed analysis of one passage; my aim here will be to show that textural detail is not merely local in its point and effect but relates to the central themes and dominant moral

[3] William Troy, "Scott Fitzgerald: The Authority of Failure," *Accent*, 1945.

attitudes expressed in the book. Analysis of prose is always liable to be cumbrous and clumsy but this very clumsiness is an oblique tribute to the dexterity and economy with which Fitzgerald achieves his effects. I take as my example a passage dealing with the end of the first of Gatsby's parties to be described in the book. The glamour and enchantment of the party, so brilliantly evoked by Fitzgerald, has here dissolved; the intoxication of night and music, champagne and youth, has vanished and the scene is closed by a dismal return to the world of sober reality, or more precisely, to the disenchanted world of the hangover. The party is over; it is time to go home. Here is the passage:

> I looked around. *Most of the remaining women were now having fights with men said to be their husbands.* (1) Even Jordan's party, the quartet from East Egg, were rent asunder by dissension. *One of the men was talking with curious intensity to a young actress,* (2) and his wife, after attempting to laugh at the situation in a dignified and indifferent way, broke down entirely and resorted to flank attacks—at intervals she appeared suddenly at his side like an angry diamond, and hissed "You promised!" into his ear.
>
> The reluctance to go home was not confined to wayward men. *The hall was at present occupied by two deplorably sober men and their highly indignant wives.* (3) The wives were sympathizing with each other in slightly raised voices.
>
> "Whenever he sees I'm having a good time he wants to go home."
>
> "Never heard anything so selfish in my life."
>
> "We're always the first ones to leave."
>
> "So are we."
>
> "Well, we're almost the last tonight," said one of the men sheepishly. "The orchestra left half an hour ago."
>
> *In spite of the wives' agreement that such malevolence was beyond credibility, the dispute ended in a short struggle, and both wives were lifted, kicking, into the night.* (4)

At first we might seem to be concerned with a piece of merely slick, glossy writing; the simile, *like an angry diamond,* is perhaps a little too smart, a little too consciously clever and contrived; it trembles on the verge of preciosity. But leaving this aside, we may see how most of the main themes are touched on tangentially in what appear to be superficial and cynical comments. I wish to concentrate on the four short passages I have, for convenient reference, italicized and numbered.

(1) This sentence, apart from the obvious implication about the sexual morality of such a society, relates as well to the rootlessness and transience of these people, the lack of any stable relationship—a point I shall discuss later. It is also one strand in the complex network of gossip, rumour and innuendo which fills the whole book.

(2) Here, the intensity is in one sense anything but curious; the relationship implied is obvious; but in another sense the intensity *is* curious in that this is a society which is flippant and cynical, gay and hedonistic, but definitely not intense in its feeling for anyone or anything; as such, it contrasts with the real intensity of the outsider who is its host, with the passion of Gatsby's dream of Daisy.

(3) Here Fitzgerald is employing a common satirical device; he is enforcing his morality by pretending to accept its opposite as the norm—sobriety becomes deplorable. Further, however, the syntactical balance of the sentence leads us to infer a causal relationship between the balanced parts—the wives are indignant because the men are sober and want, therefore, to go home. We may link this with another device Fitzgerald often uses, namely, his method of making his point by simple juxtaposition without any comment. It is a method akin to Pope's in, for example, the often-quoted line:

Puffs, powders, patches, Bibles, billets-doux.

In a catalogue like this each object assumes an equal status, and the fact that a bible may be seen as sharing the importance or triviality of its context is comment enough on the society in which such an equivalence can be contemplated. So in Fitzgerald. For example, we are told that Tom and Daisy drifted around "wherever people played polo and were rich together." There, the juxtaposition of playing a game and being wealthy indicates the superficiality and frivolity of the rich. One finds a rather different effect achieved when Fitzgerald describes Gatsby's party: "In his blue gardens men and girls came and went like moths among the whisperings and the champagne *and the stars,*" where the phrase I have italicized illuminates by contrast the transience and evanescence of the whisperings, champagne and the moth-like men and girls.

(4) Here Fitzgerald achieves yet another effect, this time by a contrast of diction. The first half of the sentence, with its polysyllabic abstraction, approaches the inflation of mock-heroic; it is promptly deflated by the abrupt, racy description of action in the second half of the sentence.

Such analysis may seem to be breaking a butterfly upon a wheel, but the fact that it is so laboured is merely the result of trying to bring to a conscious formulation something that we respond to immediately and unconsciously in our casual reading of the novel. But it will have served its purpose if it helps to show that beneath the gaiety and wit of his prose Fitzgerald is maintaining a light but insistent moral pressure and is guiding and preparing our attitudes and responses so that we shall make a correct evaluation when the need arises. All this is done through his manipulation of the point of view afforded us by the narrator, Nick Carraway, who acts as the moral seismograph of the novel's uneasiness, premonitory quakings and final eruption into catastrophe.

We may extend this analysis by noticing how key phrases are repeated subtly but insistently and how the work is so admirably organized, so intact as well as compact, that any one of these phrases inevitably leads to another and then to another, so that wherever the reader enters the book—whatever aspect of it he chooses to emphasize —his attention is engaged in a series of ever-widening perspectives until the whole of the novel is encompassed. Let us take, quite arbitrarily, the word *restless;* if we follow up this tiny and apparently insignificant verbal clue we shall find that it leads us swiftly and decisively to the heart of the book. Any one of a dozen other starting-points would do the same. Consider these examples:

(a) Of Nick: "A little later I participated in that delayed Teutonic migration known as the Great War. I enjoyed the counter-raid so thoroughly that I came back restless."

(b) Of Tom, surveying his Long Island estate: " 'I've got a nice place here,' he said, his eyes flashing about restlessly." Later he is seen "hovering restlessly about the room."

(c) Of Jordan Baker: "Her body asserted itself with a restless movement of her knee, and she stood up."

These instances of our chosen key-word, all occurring within the first twenty pages of the novel, are complicated and supplemented by other phrases suggesting sudden movement, either jerky and impulsive, as of Tom:

Wedging his tense arm imperatively under mine, Tom Buchanan compelled me from the room as though he were moving a checker to another square.

or, by contrast, of Jordan:

She yawned and with a series of rapid, deft movements stood up into the room.

We may notice again how Fitzgerald often obtains his local effects; how in the second example the unusual preposition *into* gives a peculiar force to the sentence, how, in the description of Tom, the word *imperatively* interacts with the word *compelled* so that the latter also contains the sense of *impels* and how the simile of checkers gives one the sense of manipulation, a sense which expands into the whole complex of human relationships, plots, intrigues and dreams that fills the novel.

In this context, repose is seen as a strained effort, the result of which is precarious; thus Jordan

> was extended full length at her end of the divan, completely motionless, and with her chin raised a little, as if she were balancing something on it which was likely to fall.

Even the house seems unable to stay still:

> A breeze blew through the room, blew curtains in at one end and out the other like pale flags, twisting them up toward the frosted wedding-cake of the ceiling, and then *rippled over the wine-coloured rug, making a shadow on it as a wind does on the sea.*

> The only completely stationary object in the room was an enormous couch on which two young women *were buoyed up,* as though upon an *anchored* balloon. They were both in white, and their dresses were *rippling* and fluttering as though they had just been blown back in after a short flight around the house. I must have stood for a few minutes listening to the whip and snap of the curtains and the *groan of a picture on the wall.*

In this passage one verbal trail intersects another and it is by this continual criss-cross of phrases and images that Fitzgerald achieves the effect I have already mentioned of a widening perspective. The image here, submerged beneath the surface elaboration of the prose and coming out in the phrases I have italicized is not, as one might expect, of flight but rather one of ships and the sea; a complicated image, a double exposure, so to speak, in which the whole house is seen as a ship groaning in the wind, with its flags flying, and at the same time in which the divan is a kind of ship within ship, upon the wine-coloured sea of the rug. The connecting link between the two aspects of the image is, of course, the activity and effect of the wind; both curtains and dresses ripple. There is a great deal that could be said about this kind of submerged activity in the novel to which we respond unconsciously in a casual nonanalytical reading of it; for the moment, however, I am concerned only to note how the idea of restlessness is linked with the idea of the sea. We will return to this connection shortly: we may first notice how this restlessness expands and fills the opening of the book, especially the scene of the first dinner party at the Buchanans.

The dinner begins quietly enough "with a bantering inconsequence that was never quite chatter" but the inconsequence is soon out of control; people are continually interrupting each other, changing the subject, Tom becomes vehement. Daisy is possessed by "turbulent emotions," the air is full of whispers, implications, innuendos, people are always shifting around, the "shrill metallic urgency" of the telephone

is never absent for long. The following passage is a good example of
the general atmosphere:

> Miss Baker and I exchanged a short glance consciously devoid of mean-
> ing. I was about to speak when she sat up alertly and said "Sh!" in a
> warning voice. A subdued impassioned murmur was audible in the
> room beyond, and Miss Baker leaned forward unashamed, trying to
> hear. The murmur trembled on the verge of coherence, sank down,
> mounted excitedly and then ceased altogether.

This atmosphere is most completely expressed in Nick's feeling about
Daisy:

> as though the whole evening had been a trick of some sort to exact a con-
> tributory emotion from me. I waited, and sure enough, in a moment she
> looked at me with a smirk on her lovely face, as if she had asserted her
> membership in a rather distinguished secret society to which she and
> Tom belonged.

Just as this passage anticipates the moment after the catastrophe
when Daisy and Tom look as though they are conspiring together, so
the whole scene prepares us for the picture of Tom's affair with Mrs.
Wilson which by its squalor, its triviality, its commonplaceness is a
preparatory contrast with the naive grandeur of Gatsby's schemes to
meet Daisy once again. The atmosphere of the dinner, as I have tried to
describe it, is thus established as part of the emotional and moral
climate of the whole book. But it is much more than mere scene-setting;
let us follow out a little further some of the implications of the restlessness motif. Ultimately this derives from the rootlessness of those
people; they are strangers not only to their own country but also to
their past. They live in houses that may be palaces but are certainly
not homes; their intellectual ideas are shoddy and their moral attitudes
to life are at best the detritus of a collapsed social framework, second-
hand and conventionally assumed, so that Nick is tempted to laugh
at Tom's abrupt "transition from libertine to prig" while the most he
can find to admire is the "hardy scepticism" of Jordan Baker.

All the implications of this rootlessness radiate from another key-
word, *drifting,* and we may notice how Fitzgerald, early in the book,
links this idea with the idea of restlessness, when he writes of Daisy
and Tom:

> Why they came back East I don't know. They had spent a year in
> France for no particular reason, and then drifted here and there un-
> restfully wherever people played polo and were rich together.

Each example of this kind of thing, when taken in isolation, may
seem neutral, empty of metaphorical richness, but the interaction of

these two ideas is so insistent that each tiny accretion of phrase and image builds up a powerful cumulative charge. We have already seen the image of the sea at work beneath a passage of descriptive prose, but it extends with a deceptive casualness throughout the whole book; at Gatsby's parties Nick notes "the sea-change of faces and voices and colour" and is "rather ill at ease among swirls and eddies of people"; at these parties Tom says one meets "all kinds of crazy fish" and later protests that people will "throw everything overboard." Examples could be multiplied but we need only notice the recurrence of the metaphors of sea, drifting and voyaging in two crucial passages. The first is towards the end of Nick's prefatory comments:

> No—Gatsby turned out all right at the end; it is what preyed on Gatsby, what foul dust floated in the wake of his dreams that temporarily closed out my interest in the aborted sorrows and short-winded hopes of men.

and in the very last words of the book: "So we beat on, boats against the current, borne back ceaselessly into the past."

I would like to suggest that far below the surface of *The Great Gatsby*—below the particular interest of the narrative, below Fitzgerald's analysis of society, below even the allegedly "mythic" qualities of the book—is a potent cliché, a commonplace of universal human experience to which we all respond. To say one of the bases of the novel is a cliché is not to dispraise Fitzgerald—most great art is built upon similar platitudes and it is probably why the novel is alive for another age than Fitzgerald's and for non-Americans—what we should admire is the way in which he has refreshed the cliché, given it a new accession of life in his story. The cliché I refer to is easily summed up; in the words of a popular hymn it is this:

> Time, like an ever-rolling stream,
> Bears all its sons away;
> They fly forgotten, as a dream
> Dies at the opening day.

The simple truth of this fact of life is everywhere implicit in the texture of the novel, and sometimes it is more than implicit. The appropriateness of the way in which Nick records the names of all those people who went to Gatsby's house that summer has often been remarked:

> Once I wrote down on the empty spaces of a time-table the names of those who came to Gatsby's house that Summer. It is an old time-table now, disintegrating at its folds, and headed "This schedule in effect July 5th, 1922."

There could be no more decorous memorial to those "men and girls" who "came and went like moths among the whisperings and the champagne and the stars."

It is essential to Gatsby's tragic illusion, his belief in "the unreality of reality; a promise that the rock of the world was founded securely on a fairy's wing," that he should deny this fact of life and try to make the ever rolling stream flow back up-hill.

"I wouldn't ask too much of her," I ventured. "You can't repeat the the past." "Can't repeat the past?" he cried incredulously. "Why of course you can!"

It is not insignificant that Nick should be so acutely aware of the passing of time, while in this context Gatsby's apology, "I'm sorry about the clock" acquires a new level of unconscious ironic meaning. This has been stressed often enough before; the point I wish to make is that the theme, basic to *The Great Gatsby*, is not merely adumbrated, is not merely translated into terms of narrative and character, but is also expressed in the very texture of the prose, in the phrases and images, for example, which centre on words like *restless* and *drifting*. Thus the moral attitude of Nick is conveyed in precisely these terms. We may note in passing that Nick is not the fixed, static point of view some critics have supposed him; he is not the detached observer but is deeply implicated in the story he is telling and his attitude evolves and changes as the story progresses; in a sense what *The Great Gatsby* is about is what happens to Nick. At the outset he "began to like New York, the racy adventurous feel of it at night, and the satisfaction that the constant flicker of men and women and machines gives to the restless eye." The attractiveness and glamour of Gatsby's parties needs no stressing but Nick begins to feel oppressed and uneasy at the "many-coloured, many-keyed commotion." And his reaction after the catastrophe is naturally expressed in an antithesis to the terms already established.

When I came back from the East last autumn I felt that I wanted the world to be in uniform and at a sort of moral attention forever.

Similarly, the ambiguity of Gatsby himself comes over to us in these terms. He is not the simple antithesis of Tom and Daisy; he is implicated in their kind of corruption too, and his dream is proved hollow not only by the inadequacy of the actual correlative—that is, Daisy—to the hunger of his aspiring imagination, but also by the means he uses to build up the gaudy fabric of his vision. He, too, shares in the restlessness of the actual world which will defeat his ideal, Platonic conceptions:

This quality was continually breaking through his punctilious manner in the shape of restlessness. He was never quite still; there was always a tapping foot somewhere or the impatient opening and closing of a hand.

and a little later he tells Nick:

> "You see, I usually find myself among strangers because I drift here and there trying to forget the sad thing that happened to me."

This note of drifting is frequently reiterated in connection with Gatsby but it does not, as in the case of Daisy and Tom, remain unqualified; Gatsby comes out all right at the end. What we remember about him is not the restlessness or the drifting but "an unbroken series of successful gestures," Gatsby standing in the moonlight outside the Buchanans' house, rapt in "the sacredness of the vigil"; Gatsby in his own temple-cum-roadhouse between "the great doors, endowing with complete isolation the figure of the host, who stood on the porch, his hand up in a formal gesture of farewell," or above all, Gatsby stretching out his arms towards the green light that is the vain promise of his future. We remember these formal poses as something theatrical or religious, but they *are* poses, moments of suspended time, something static and as such are the stylistic equivalents of Gatsby's attempt to impose his dream upon reality, his effort to make the ever-rolling stream stand still. We remember Gatsby not as drifting but as voyaging to some end and it is this sense, hinted at all the way through the book, which gives impetus to that imaginative leap whereby we encompass the ironic contrast between Gatsby and Columbus or those Dutch sailors in that moment when "man must have held his breath in the presence of this continent, compelled into an aesthetic contemplation he neither understood nor desired, face to face for the last time in history with something commensurate to his capacity for wonder."

Thus, starting with the idea of restlessness and going by way of its enlargement into the idea of drifting we are brought to face the largest issues that the novel propounds. This is, of course, not the only—or even the most important—strand in the textural pattern of the whole; any one of a dozen other starting points might have been taken—the contrast between East and West, for example, the subtle choreography of the terms *reality* and *unreality,* the functional role of the machine which enlarges to provide metaphors for the emotional and moral life, the religious overtones that some critics have noted, or the ideas of money and value. All of these combine and interact to give *The Great Gatsby* its satisfying depth and richness of suggestion without which the themes so often abstracted for discussion would lack both definition and reverberant power and the novel would fail to achieve that quality which Mark Schorer has described as "language as used to create a certain texture and tone which in themselves state and define themes and meanings; or language, the counters of our ordinary speech, as forced, through conscious manipulation, into all those larger meanings which our ordinary speech almost never intends." [4]

[4] Mark Schorer, "Technique as Discovery," *Hudson Review*, Spring, 1948.

PART TWO

View Points

Maxwell Perkins: Letter to F. Scott Fitzgerald

NOVEMBER 20, 1924

DEAR SCOTT:

I think you have every kind of right to be proud of this book.[1] It is an extraordinary book, suggestive of all sorts of thoughts and moods. You adopted exactly the right method of telling it, that of employing a narrator who is more of a spectator than an actor: this puts the reader upon a point of observation on a higher level than that on which the characters stand and at a distance that gives perspective. In no other way could your irony have been so immensely effective, nor the reader have been enabled so strongly to feel at times the strangeness of human circumstance in a vast heedless universe. In the eyes of Dr. Eckleberg various readers will see different significances; but their presence gives a superb touch to the whole thing: great unblinking eyes, expressionless, looking down upon the human scene. It's magnificent!

I could go on praising the book and speculating on its various elements, and means, but points of criticism are more important now. I think you are right in feeling a certain slight sagging in chapters six and seven, and I don't know how to suggest a remedy. I hardly doubt that you will find one and I am only writing to say that I think it does need something to hold up here to the pace set, and ensuing. I have only two actual criticisms:

One is that among a set of characters marvelously palpable and vital —I would know Tom Buchanan if I met him on the street and would avoid him—Gatsby is somewhat vague. The reader's eyes can never quite focus upon him, his outlines are dim. Now everything about Gatsby is more or less a mystery, i.e. more or less vague, and this may be somewhat of an artistic intention, but I think it is mistaken.

"To F. Scott Fitzgerald" by Maxwell Perkins. From Editor to Author, the Letters of Maxwell Perkins, *ed. John Hall Wheelock (New York: Charles Scribner's Sons, 1950), pp. 38-41. Copyright © 1950 by Charles Scribner's Sons. Reprinted by permission of the publisher.*

[1] *The Great Gatsby,* Charles Scribner's Sons, 1925.

Couldn't *he* be physically described as distinctly as the others, and couldn't you add one or two characteristics like the use of that phrase "old sport"—not verbal, but physical ones, perhaps. I think that for some reason or other a reader—this was true of Mr. Scribner[2] and of Louise[3]—gets an idea that Gatsby is a much older man than he is, although you have the writer say that he is little older than himself. But this would be avoided if on his first appearance he was seen as vividly as Daisy and Tom are, for instance—and I do not think your scheme would be impaired if you made him so.

The other point is also about Gatsby: his career must remain mysterious, of course. But in the end you make it pretty clear that his wealth came through his connection with Wolfsheim. You also suggest this much earlier. Now almost all readers numerically are going to be puzzled by his having all this wealth and are going to feel entitled to an explanation. To give a distinct and definite one would be, of course, utterly absurd. It did occur to me, though, that you might here and there interpolate some phrases, and possibly incidents, little touches of various kinds, that would suggest that he was in some active way mysteriously engaged. You do have him called on the telephone, but couldn't he be seen once or twice consulting at his parties with people of some sort of myterious significance, from the political, the gambling, the sporting world, or whatever it may be. I know I am floundering, but that fact may help you to see what I mean. The *total* lack of an explanation through so large a part of the story does seem to me a defect—or not of an explanation, but of the suggestion of an explanation. I wish you were here so I could talk about it to you, for then I know I could at least make you understand what I mean. What Gatsby did ought never to be definitely imparted, even if it could be. Whether he was an innocent tool in the hands of somebody else, or to what degree he was this, ought not to be explained. But if some sort of business activity of his were simply adumbrated, it would lend further probability to that part of the story.

There is one other point: in giving deliberately Gatsby's biography, when he gives it to the narrator, you do depart from the method of the narrative in some degree, for otherwise almost everything is told, and beautifully told, in the regular flow of it, in the succession of events or in accompaniment with them. But you can't avoid the biography altogether. I thought you might find ways to let the truth of some of his claims like "Oxford" and his army career come out, bit by bit, in the course of actual narrative. I mention the point anyway, for consideration in this interval before I send the proofs.

[2] Charles Scribner, Senior (1854-1930), president of Charles Scribner's Sons.
[3] Mrs. Maxwell E. Perkins.

The general brilliant quality of the book makes me ashamed to make even these criticisms. The amount of meaning you get into a sentence, the dimensions and intensity of the impression you make a paragraph carry, are most extraordinary. The manuscript is full of phrases which make a scene blaze with life. If one enjoyed a rapid railroad journey I would compare the number and vividness of pictures your living words suggest, to the living scenes disclosed in that way. It seems, in reading, a much shorter book than it is, but it carries the mind through a series of experiences that one would think would require a book of three times its length.

The presentation of Tom, his place, Daisy and Jordan, and the unfolding of their characters is unequaled so far as I know. The description of the valley of ashes adjacent to the lovely country, the conversation and the action in Myrtle's apartment, the marvelous catalogue of those who came to Gatsby's house—these are such things as make a man famous. And all these things, the whole pathetic episode, you have given a place in time and space, for with the help of T. J. Eckleberg and by an occasional glance at the sky, or the sea, or the city, you have imparted a sort of sense of eternity. You once told me you were not a *natural writer*—my God! You have plainly mastered the craft, of course; but you needed far more than craftsmanship for this.

As ever,

Conrad Aiken: F. Scott Fitzgerald

In *The Great Gatsby* . . . Mr. Fitzgerald has written a highly colored and brilliant little novel which, by grace of one cardinal virtue, quite escapes the company of most contemporary American fiction—it has excellence of form. It is not great, it is not large, it is not strikingly subtle; but it is well imagined and shaped, it moves swiftly and neatly, its scene is admirably seized and admirably matched with the theme, and its hard bright tone is entirely original. Technically, it appears to owe much to the influence of the cinema; and perhaps also something to Henry James—a peculiar conjunction, but not so peculiar if one reflects on the flash-backs and close-ups and paralleled themes of that "little experiment in the style of Gyp," *The Awkward Age.* Mr. Fitzgerald's publishers call *The Great Gatsby* a satire. This is deceptive. It is only incidentally a satire, it is only in the *setting* that it is satirical,

"*F. Scott Fitzgerald*" *by Conrad Aiken. From* A Reviewer's ABC (*New York: Meridian Books, 1958*), *pp. 209-10. The essay first appeared in 1926. Copyright © 1958 by Conrad Aiken. Reprinted by permission of Brandt & Brandt.*

and in the tone provided by the minor characters. The story itself, and the main figure, are tragic, and it is precisely the fantastic vulgarity of the scene which gives to the excellence of Gatsby's soul its finest bouquet, and to his tragic fate its sharpest edge. All of Mr. Fitzgerald's people are real—but Gatsby comes close to being superb. He is betrayed to us slowly and skillfully, and with a keen tenderness which in the end makes his tragedy a deeply moving one. By so much, therefore, *The Great Gatsby* is better than a mere satire of manners, and better than Mr. Fitzgerald's usual sort of superficial cleverness. If only he can refrain altogether in future from the sham romanticism and sham sophistication which the magazines demand of him, and give another turn of the screw to the care with which he writes, he may well become a first-rate novelist. How deeply does he feel? That is the question, a question we do not ask of Miss Loos or Mr. Lardner.

Peter Quennell: The Great Gatsby

It would be doing Scott Fitzgerald a grave injustice to suggest that his novel was merely an essay in social satire, with special reference to the abuses of the capitalist system. His strictures on the worlds he describes are implied, not stated. *The Great Gatsby* is one of the most typical and also one of the most brilliant products of that exciting, disappointing period which witnessed the birth and extinction of so many hopes and crashed at last into the doldrums of a vast depression. It is a period piece with an unusual degree of permanent value, having the sadness and the remote jauntiness of a Gershwin tune, the same touches of slightly bogus romanticism—"the stiff tinny drip of the banjoes on the lawn"; the headlights of departing cars which wheel like long golden antennae across the obscurity of the "soft black morning"—the same nostalgic appeal to be taken seriously, a plea that in Scott Fitzgerald's case has, I think, succeeded. A large number of American mannerisms start with Scott Fitzgerald (who somehow never repeated that early triumph, though many of his long short stories are well worth reading) and not a few modern novelists are his unconscious imitators. Today when the Bum is a best-selling hero—the Share-Cropper, the vagrant Okie, the landless Poor White—it is refreshing to read this romantic tract on the sorrows of Dives.

"The Great Gatsby" by *Peter Quennell. From* The New Statesman and Nation, *XXI (February 1, 1941), 112. Copyright © 1941 by the Statesman and Nation Publishing Company. Reprinted by permission of the publisher.*

F. Scott Fitzgerald: Letter to Edmund Wilson

[1925]
14 Rue de Tillsit
Paris, France

Dear Bunny:

Thanks for your letter about the book.* I was awfully happy that you liked it and that you approved of the design. The worst fault in it, I think is a BIG FAULT: I gave no account (and had no feeling about or knowledge of) the emotional relations between Gatsby and Daisy from the time of their reunion to the catastrophe. However the lack is so astutely concealed by the retrospect of Gatsby's past and by blankets of excellent prose that no one has noticed it—though everyone has felt the lack and called it by another name. Mencken said (in a most enthusiastic letter received today) that the only fault was that the central story was trivial and a sort of anecdote (that is because he has forgotten his admiration for Conrad and adjusted himself to the sprawling novel) and I felt that what he really missed was the lack of any emotional backbone at the very height of it.

Without making any invidious comparisons between Class A and Class C, if my novel is an anecdote, so is *The Brothers Karamazoff*. From one angle the latter could be reduced into a detective story. However the letters from you and Mencken have compensated me for the fact that of all the reviews, even the most enthusiastic, not one had the slightest idea what the book was about and for the even more depressing fact that it was in comparison with the others a financial failure (after I'd turned down fifteen thousand for the serial rights!) I wonder what Rosenfeld thought of it.

I looked up Hemminway. He is taking me to see Gertrude Stein tomorrow. This city is full of Americans—most of them former friends—whom we spend most of our time dodging, not because we don't want to see them but because Zelda's only just well and I've got to work; and they seem to be incapable of any sort of conversation not composed of semi-malicious gossip about New York courtesy celebrities. I've gotten to like France. We've taken a swell apartment until January. I'm filled

---

"*To Edmund Wilson*" by *F. Scott Fitzgerald. From* The Crack-Up, *ed. Edmund Wilson (New York: New Directions Publishing Corporation, 1945), pp. 270-71, and from* The Letters of *F. Scott Fitzgerald, ed. Andrew Turnbull, and* The Bodley Head Scott Fitzgerald, *III (London: The Bodley Head, 1945). Copyright © 1945 by New Directions. Reprinted by permission of the publishers.*
* *The Great Gatsby.*

with disgust for Americans in general after two weeks sight of the ones in Paris—these preposterous, pushing women and girls who assume that you have any personal interest in them, who have all (so they say) read James Joyce and who simply adore Mencken. I suppose we're no worse than anyone, only contact with other races brings out all our worse qualities. If I had anything to do with creating the manners of the contemporary American girl I certainly made a botch of the job.

I'd love to see you. God. I could give you some laughs. There's no news except that Zelda and I think we're pretty good, as usual, only more so.

Scott

Thanks again for your cheering letter.

Edith Wharton: Letter to F. Scott Fitzgerald

Pavillon Colombe
St. Brice-Sous-Forêt (S&O)
Gare: Sarcelles

June 8, 1925

Dear Mr. Fitzgerald,

I have been wandering for the last weeks and found your novel—with its friendly dedication—awaiting me here on my arrival, a few days ago.

I am touched at your sending me a copy, for I feel that to your generation, which has taken such a flying leap into the future, I must represent the literary equivalent of tufted furniture & gas chandeliers. So you will understand that it is in a spirit of sincere deprecation that I shall venture, in a few days, to offer you in return the last product of my manufactory.

Meanwhile, let me say at once how much I like Gatsby, or rather His Book, & how great a leap I think you have taken this time—in advance upon your previous work. My present quarrel with you is only this: that to make Gatsby really Great, you ought to have given us his early career (not from the cradle—but from his visit to the yacht, if not before) instead of a short résumé of it. That would have situated him, & made his final tragedy a tragedy instead of a "fait divers" for the morning papers.

"To F. Scott Fitzgerald" by Edith Wharton. From The Crack-Up, *ed.* Edmund Wilson *(New York: New Directions Publishing Corporation, 1945), pp. 309-10. Copyright © 1945 by New Directions. Reprinted by permission of New Directions and A. Watkins, Inc.*

But you'll tell me that's the old way, & consequently not *your* way; & meanwhile, it's enough to make this reader happy to have met your *perfect* Jew, & the limp Wilson, & assisted at that seedy orgy in the Buchanan flat, with the dazed puppy looking on. Every bit of that is masterly—but the lunch with Hildeshiem,* and his every appearance afterward, make me augur still greater things!—Thank you again.

Yrs. Sincerely,
Edith Wharton

I have left hardly space to ask if you & Mrs. Fitzgerald won't come to lunch or tea some day this week. Do call me up.

Richard Chase: From "Three Novels of Manners"

No one seems to know what T. S. Eliot meant when he wrote Fitzgerald that *Gatsby* was the first step forward the American novel had made since Henry James. The statement seems meaningful, however, if we compare *Gatsby* with James's only novel of similar theme, *The American.* Christopher Newman is a more relaxed, less willful, and less self-destined figure than Gatsby, but he comes of a similarly legendary America, makes a great deal of money, and vainly pursues a woman who is the flower of a high world forever closed to him. James, however, is content with his pleasure in the odd angularities of the legend of the successful American. And he sends Newman home, baffled and saddened by his rejection but not mortally hurt. It is a part of the fate of both Newman and Gatsby that they have information with which they could avenge themselves on their highly placed antagonists and that out of magnanimity they both refuse to do so.

But Fitzgerald has made more of the legend. For whereas Newman remains an odd though appealing stick of a man Gatsby has a tragic recklessness about him, an inescapably vivid and memorable destiny. He has something of that almost divine insanity we find in Hamlet or Julien Sorel or Don Quixote. Fitzgerald's great feat was to have opened out this possibility and to have made his American hero act in a drama where none had acted before. For although there had been reckless and doomed semilegendary heroes in American fiction, none had been made to play his part in a realistically presented *social* situation. Fitzgerald

---

"From 'Three Novels of Manners'" in The American Novel and its Tradition, *by Richard Chase (Garden City, N.Y.: Doubleday Anchor Books, 1957), pp. 166-67. Copyright © 1957 by Richard Chase. Reprinted by permission of Doubleday & Company, Inc.*

* The name should be Wolfsheim. Hildesheim was misspelled Hildeshiem in the first edition of *The Great Gatsby.*

opened out the possibility, but scarcely more. It was not in him to emulate except for a brilliant moment the greatest art.

F. Scott Fitzgerald: Introduction to *The Great Gatsby*

Introduction

To one who has spent his professional life in the world of fiction the request to "write an introduction" offers many facets of temptation. The present writer succumbs to one of them; with as much equanimity as he can muster, he will discuss the critics among us, trying to revolve as centripetally as possible about the novel which comes hereafter in this volume.

To begin with, I must say that I have no cause to grumble about the "press" of any book of mine. If Jack (who liked my last book) didn't like this one—well then John (who despised my last book) *did* like it; so it all mounts up to the same total. But I think the writers of my time were spoiled in that regard, living in generous days when there was plenty of space on the page for endless ratiocination about fiction —a space largely created by Mencken because of his disgust for what passed as criticism before he arrived and made his public. They were encouraged by his bravery and his tremendous and profound love of letters. In his case, the jackals are already tearing at what they imprudently regard as a moribund lion, but I don't think many men of my age can regard him without reverence, nor fail to regret that he got off the train. To any new effort by a new man he brought an attitude; he made many mistakes—such as his early undervaluation of Hemingway —but he came equipped; he never had to go back for his tools.

And now that he has abandoned American fiction to its own devices, there is no one to take his place. If the present writer had seriously to attend some of the efforts of political diehards to tell him the values of a métier he has practised since boyhood—well, then, babies, you can take this number out and shoot him at dawn.

But all that is less discouraging, in the past few years, than the growing cowardice of the reviewers. Underpaid and overworked, they seem not to care for books, and it has been saddening recently to see young talents in fiction expire from sheer lack of a stage to act on: West, McHugh and many others.

I'm circling closer to my theme song, which is: that I'd like to communicate to such of them who read this novel a healthy cynicism toward contemporary reviews. Without undue vanity one can permit oneself a suit of chain mail in any profession. Your pride is all you have, and if you let it be tampered with by a man who has a dozen prides to tamper with before lunch, you are promising yourself a lot of disappointments that a hard-boiled professional has learned to spare himself.

This novel is a case in point. Because the pages weren't loaded with big names of big things and the subject not concerned with farmers (who were the heroes of the moment), there was easy judgment exercised that had nothing to do with criticism but was simply an attempt on the part of men who had few chances of self-expression to express themselves. How anyone could take up the responsibility of being a novelist without a sharp and concise attitude about life is a puzzle to me. How a critic could assume a point of view which included twelve variant aspects of the social scene in a few hours seems something too dinosaurean to loom over the awful loneliness of a young author.

To circle nearer to this book, one woman, who could hardly have written a coherent letter in English, described it as a book that one read only as one goes to the movies around the corner. That type of criticism is what a lot of young writers are being greeted with, instead of any appreciation of the world of imagination in which they (the writers) have been trying, with greater or lesser success, to live—the world that Mencken made stable in the days when he was watching over us.

Now that this book is being reissued, the author would like to say that never before did one try to keep his artistic conscience as pure as during the ten months put into doing it. Reading it over one can see how it could have been improved—yet without feeling guilty of any discrepancy from the truth, as far as I saw it; truth or rather the *equivalent* of the truth, the attempt at honesty of imagination. I had just re-read Conrad's preface to *The Nigger,* and I had recently been kidded half haywire by critics who felt that my material was such as to preclude all dealing with mature persons in a mature world. But, my God! it was my material, and it was all I had to deal with.

What I cut out of it both physically and emotionally would make another novel!

I think it is an honest book, that is to say, that one used none of one's virtuosity to get an effect, and, to boast again, one soft-pedalled the emotional side to avoid the tears leaking from the socket of the left eye, or the large false face peering around the corner of a character's head.

If there is a clear conscience, a book can survive—at least in one's feelings about it. On the contrary, if one has a guilty conscience, one reads what one wants to hear out of reviews. In addition, if one is young and willing to learn, almost all reviews have a value, even the ones that seem unfair.

The present writer has always been a "natural" for his profession, in so much that he can think of nothing he could have done as efficiently as to have lived deeply in the world of imagination. There are plenty other people constituted as he is, for giving expression to intimate explorations, the:

—Look—this is here!

—I saw this under my eyes.

—*This* is the way it was!

—No, it was like this.

"Look! Here is that drop of blood I told you about."

—"Stop everything! Here is the flash of that girl's eyes, here is the reflection that will always come back to me from the memory of her eyes.

—"If one chooses to find that face again in the non-refracting surface of a washbowl, if one chooses to make the image more obscure with a little sweat, it should be the business of the critic to recognize the intention.

—"No one felt like this before—says the young writer—but *I* felt like this; I have a pride akin to a soldier going into battle; without knowing whether there will be anybody there, to distribute medals or even to record it."

But remember, also, young man: you are not the first person who has ever been alone and alone.

F. Scott Fitzgerald

Baltimore, Md.
August, 1934.

Lionel Trilling: F. Scott Fitzgerald

It is hard to overestimate the benefit which came to Fitzgerald from his having consciously placed himself in the line of the great. He was a "natural," but he did not have the contemporary American novelist's belief that if he compares himself with the past masters, or if he takes thought—which, for a writer, means really knowing what his predecessors have done—he will endanger the integrity of his natural gifts. To read Fitzgerald's letters to his daughter—they are among the best and

"*F. Scott Fitzgerald*" *by Lionel Trilling. From* The Liberal Imagination (*New York: The Viking Press, Inc., 1950; London: Martin Secker & Warburg, Ltd., 1950*), *pp. 250-54. Copyright © 1945 by Lionel Trilling. Reprinted by permission of the publishers.*

most affecting letters I know—and to catch the tone in which he speaks about the literature of the past, or to read the notebooks he faithfully kept, indexing them as Samuel Butler had done, and to perceive how continuously he thought about literature, is to have some clue to the secret of the continuing power of Fitzgerald's work.

The Great Gatsby, for example, after a quarter-century is still as fresh as when it first appeared; it has even gained in weight and relevance, which can be said of very few American books of its time. This, I think, is to be attributed to the specifically intellectual courage with which it was conceived and executed, a courage which implies Fitzgerald's grasp —both in the sense of awareness and of appropriation—of the traditional resources available to him. Thus, *The Great Gatsby* has its interest as a record of contemporary manners, but this might only have served to date it, did not Fitzgerald take the given moment of history as something more than a mere circumstance, did he not, in the manner of the great French novelists of the nineteenth century, seize the given moment as a moral fact. The same boldness of intellectual grasp accounts for the success of the conception of its hero—Gatsby is said by some to be not quite credible, but the question of any literal credibility he may or may not have becomes trivial before the large significance he implies. For Gatsby, divided between power and dream, comes inevitably to stand for America itself. Ours is the only nation that prides itself upon a dream and gives its name to one, "the American dream." We are told that "the truth was that Jay Gatsby of West Egg, Long Island, sprang from his Platonic conception of himself. He was a son of God—a phrase which, if it means anything, means just that—and he must be about His Father's business, the service of a vast, vulgar, and meritricious beauty." Clearly it is Fitzgerald's intention that our mind should turn to the thought of the nation that has sprung from its "Platonic conception" of itself. To the world it is anomalous in America, just as in the novel it is anomalous in Gatsby, that so much raw power should be haunted by envisioned romance. Yet in that anomaly lies, for good or bad, much of the truth of our national life, as, at the present moment, we think about it:

Then, if the book grows in weight of significance with the years, we can be sure that this could not have happened had its form and style not been as right as they are. Its form is ingenious—with the ingenuity, however, not of craft but of intellectual intensity. The form, that is, is not the result of careful "plotting"—the form of a good novel never is —but is rather the result of the necessities of the story's informing idea, which require the sharpness of radical foreshortening. Thus, it will be observed, the characters are not "developed": the wealthy and brutal Tom Buchanan, haunted by his "scientific" vision of the doom of civilization, the vaguely guilty, vaguely homosexual Jordan Baker, the dim

Wolfsheim, who fixed the World Series of 1919, are treated, we might say, as if they were ideographs, a method of economy that is reinforced by the ideographic use that is made of the Washington Heights flat, the terrible "valley of ashes" seen from the Long Island Railroad, Gatsby's incoherent parties, and the huge sordid eyes of the oculist's advertising sign. (It is a technique which gives the novel an affinity with *The Waste Land,* between whose author and Fitzgerald there existed a reciprocal admiration.) Gatsby himself, once stated, grows only in the understanding of the narrator. He is allowed to say very little in his own person. Indeed, apart from the famous "Her voice is full of money," he says only one memorable thing, but that remark is overwhelming in its intellectual audacity: when he is forced to admit that his lost Daisy did perhaps love her husband, he says, "In any case it was just personal." With that sentence he achieves an insane greatness, convincing us that he really is a Platonic conception of himself, really some sort of Son of God.

What underlies all success in poetry, what is even more important than the shape of the poem or its wit of metaphor, is the poet's voice. It either gives us confidence in what is being said or it tells us that we do not need to listen; and it carries both the modulation and the living form of what is being said. In the novel no less than in the poem, the voice of the author is the decisive factor. We are less consciously aware of it in the novel, and, in speaking of the elements of a novel's art, it cannot properly be exemplified by quotation because it is continuous and cumulative. In Fitzgerald's work the voice of his prose is of the essence of his success. We hear in it at once the tenderness toward human desire that modifies a true firmness of moral judgment. It is, I would venture to say, the normal or ideal voice of the novelist. It is characteristically modest, yet it has in it, without apology or self-consciousness, a largeness, even a stateliness, which derives from Fitzgerald's connection with tradition and with mind, from his sense of what has been done before and the demands which this past accomplishment makes. ". . . I became aware of the old island here that flowered once for Dutch sailors' eyes—a fresh green breast of the new world. Its vanished trees, the trees that had made way for Gatsby's house, had once pandered in whispers to the last and greatest of all human dreams; for a transitory and enchanted moment man must have held his breath in the presence of this continent, compelled into an aesthetic contemplation he neither understood nor desired, face to face for the last time in history with something commensurate to his capacity for wonder." Here, in the well-known passage, the voice is a little dramatic, a little *intentional,* which is not improper to a passage in climax and conclusion, but it will the better suggest in brief compass the habitual music of Fitzgerald's seriousness.

Fitzgerald lacked prudence, as his heroes did, lacked that blind instinct of self-protection which the writer needs and the American writer needs in double measure. But that is all he lacked—and it is the generous fault, even the heroic fault. He said of his Gatsby, "If personality is an unbroken series of successful gestures, there was something gorgeous about him, some heightened sensitivity to the promises of life, as if he were related to one of those intricate machines that register earthquakes ten thousand miles away. This responsiveness had nothing to do with that flabby impressionability which is dignified under the name of 'the creative temperament'—it was an extraordinary gift for hope, a romantic readiness such as I have never found in any other person and which it is not likely I shall ever find again." And it is so that we are drawn to see Fitzgerald himself as he stands in his exemplary role.

F. Scott Fitzgerald: Letter to his Daughter

June 12, 1940

I could agree with you as opposed to Dean Thompson if you were getting "B's." Then I would say: As you're not going to be a teacher or a professional scholar, don't try for "A's"—don't take the things in which you can get "A," for you can learn them yourself. Try something hard and new, and try it hard, and take what marks you can get. But you have no such margin of respectability, and this borderline business is a fret to you. Doubt and worry—you are as crippled by them as I am by my inability to handle money or my self-indulgences of the past. It is your Achilles' heel—and no Achilles' heel ever toughened by itself. It just gets more and more vulnerable. What little I've accomplished has been by the most laborious and uphill work, and I wish now I'd *never* relaxed or looked back—but said at the end of *The Great Gatsby*: "I've found my line—from now on this comes first. This is my immediate duty—without this I am nothing."

"Letter to his Daughter" by *F. Scott Fitzgerald. From* The Crack-Up, *ed. Edmund Wilson (New York: New Directions Publishing Corporation, 1945), p. 294, and from* The Letters of F. Scott Fitzgerald, *ed. Andrew Turnbull, and* The Bodley Head Scott Fitzgerald, *III (London: The Bodley Head, 1945). Copyright © 1945 by New Directions. Reprinted by permission of the publishers.*

Chronology of Important Dates

Fitzgerald	Historical and Cultural Events
1896 Fitzgerald born.	William McKinley defeats William Jennings Bryan for the Presidency.
1917 Fitzgerald leaves Princeton in fall of his senior year, enters army as second lieutenant, but remains stateside.	United States declares war on Germany. T. S. Eliot's *Prufrock* published.
1919 Fitzgerald discharged from army in February, *This Side of Paradise* accepted by Scribner's in September.	Prohibition becomes law. Sherwood Anderson's *Winesburg, Ohio* published.
1920 *This Side of Paradise* published. Fitzgerald marries Zelda Sayre.	Warren G. Harding elected President. Sinclair Lewis's *Main Street* published.
1922 *The Beautiful and Damned* published.	Published: James Joyce's *Ulysses,* Eliot's *The Waste Land.*
1923 *The Vegetable* fails in Atlantic City.	Calvin Coolidge succeeds to Presidency upon Harding's death. Hitler writes *Mein Kampf.* Published: Wallace Stevens' *Harmonium,* D. H. Lawrence's *Studies in Classical American Literature.*
1925 *The Great Gatsby* published.	Coolidge inaugurated for his first full term. Scopes trial pits Bryan against Clarence Darrow. Published: Ezra Pound's *Cantos,* Robinson Jeffers' *Roan Stallion,* Theodore Dreiser's *American Tragedy,* Sinclair Lewis's *Arrow-*

	smith, John Dos Passos' *Manhattan Transfer.*
1929	Stock market crash begins depression. Published: Thomas Wolfe's *Look Homeward Angel,* Ernest Hemingway's *Farewell to Arms,* William Faulkner's *Sound and the Fury.*
1933	Roosevelt becomes President. Prohibition repealed. Hitler becomes German Chancellor.
1934 *Tender is the Night* published.	Published: James T. Farrell's *Young Manhood of Studs Lonigan,* Henry Miller's *Tropic of Cancer.*
1939	Germany invades Poland. John Steinbeck's *Grapes of Wrath* published.
1940 Fitzgerald dies.	Germany invades Denmark, Norway, and Belgium, declares war on France and Great Britain, and occupies Paris. Axis formed between Germany, Italy, and Japan. Published: Hemingway's *For Whom the Bell Tolls,* Richard Wright's *Native Son,* Glenway Wescott's *The Pilgrim Hawk.*

Notes on the Editor and Contributors

ERNEST LOCKRIDGE is assistant professor of English at Yale University. He has published essays on Laurence Sterne and Henry James. His novel, *Hartspring Blows His Mind,* will be published in January, 1968.

CONRAD AIKEN is an outstanding American poet, critic, and novelist. Much of his criticism has been collected in *A Reviewer's ABC.*

MARIUS BEWLEY is professor of English at Rutgers, the State University, at New Brunswick, N.J. His books include *The Complex Fate: Hawthorne and Henry James* and *The Eccentric Design.* He has edited a selection of Donne's poetry and a critical anthology of English Romantic poetry.

RICHARD CHASE is the author of *Quest for Myth, Herman Melville, Emily Dickinson,* and *Walt Whitman Reconsidered.*

THOMAS A. HANZO is the author of many articles, including "Latitude and Restoration Criticism" and "Eliot and Kierkegaard."

W. J. HARVEY occupied the Chair of English in the Queen's University, Belfast, from 1965 until his death in May, 1967. He was the author of two volumes of verse, *The Uncertain Margin* and *Exile and Return,* and two works of criticism, *An Introduction to Macbeth* and *The Art of George Eliot.*

JAMES E. MILLER, JR. is professor of English at the University of Chicago. From 1960 to 1966 he was editor of *College English.* He has written books on Whitman, Melville, Fitzgerald, and J. D. Salinger; with Karl Shapiro and Bernice Slote he wrote *Start with the Sun: Studies in the Whitman Tradition.* His most recent book is *Quests Surd and Absurd.*

DAVID MINTER is assistant professor of American Studies at Rice University. His essay in this volume forms part of a book, which he is now completing, on American literature.

ROBERT ORNSTEIN is professor of English and chairman of the department at Case Western Reserve University. Most of his work has been in Shakespeare and Elizabethan drama, though he has written notes on Robert Frost and Mark Twain. He has edited a collection of essays on Shakespeare's problem comedies and co-edited anthologies of Elizabethan tragedy and comedy.

His first book, *The Moral Vision of Jacobean Tragedy,* is now in paperback, and he is completing a book on Shakespeare's history plays.

MAXWELL PERKINS was Scribner's famous editor. Among his authors were Fitzgerald, Ernest Hemingway, and Thomas Wolfe.

PETER QUENNELL, English critic, essayist, and biographer, is the author of (among other works) *Byron in Italy, Ruskin,* and *William Shakespeare.*

GARY J. SCRIMGEOUR is currently a lecturer at Indiana University. He has published articles on Galsworthy's plays, Hawthorne's *The Marble Faun,* and Defoe's *Captain Singleton.*

LIONEL TRILLING is professor of English at Columbia University. His most recent work is *Beyond Culture: Essays on Literature and Learning.*

EDITH WHARTON, the American novelist, was the author of *The Age of Innocence,* among other works of fiction.

Selected Bibliography

Beebe, Maurice, and Jackson R. Bryer, "Criticism of F. Scott Fitzgerald: A Selected Checklist," *Modern Fiction Studies*, VII (1961), 82-94.

Eble, Kenneth, "The Craft of Revision: *The Great Gatsby,*" *American Literature*, XXXVI (1964-65), 315-26. A brilliant examination of Fitzgerald's pencil draft and of his revision while the novel was in galleys. Eble uses the novel's genesis to illuminate its meaning.

Fussell, Edwin, "Fitzgerald's Brave New World," *English Literary History*, XIX (1952), 291-306. Fitzgerald's understanding and criticism of America.

Hoffman, Frederick J., ed., *The Great Gatsby: A Study*. New York: Charles Scribner's Sons, 1962. A generous selection of writing by and about Fitzgerald, with special focus on *Gatsby*.

MacKendrick, Paul L., "*The Great Gatsby* and Trimalchcio," *Classical Journal*, XLV (1950), 307-14. An excellent comparison of *Gatsby* with the *Satirae* of Petronius Arbiter.

Mizener, Arthur, *The Far Side of Paradise*. Boston: Houghton Mifflin Company, 1951. See especially pp. 169-88. This remains the best biographical and critical study of Fitzgerald.

Perosa, Sergio, *The Art of F. Scott Fitzgerald*. Ann Arbor: University of Michigan Press, 1965. Contains a full discussion of *Gatsby*.

Piper, Henry Dan, *F. Scott Fitzgerald: A Critical Portrait*. New York: Holt, Rinehart & Winston, Inc., 1965. Pages 100-154 constitute a rich treatment of *Gatsby*.

Schneider, Daniel J., "Color-Symbolism in *The Great Gatsby,*" *The University Review*, XXXI (1964), 13-18. An intelligent and highly original exploration of one of *Gatsby*'s major patterns; one of the best demonstrations of how fully Fitzgerald realized his desire to write something "intricately patterned."

Thale, Jerome, "The Narrator as Hero," *Twentieth Century Literature*, III (1957), 69-73. Compares *Gatsby* with Joseph Conrad's *Heart of Darkness*.